Design and Make
Your Own
Dollhouse Furniture

~

DESIGN AND MAKE
YOUR OWN
DOLLHOUSE FURNITURE

~

HEADLEY HOLGATE AND PAMELA RUDDOCK

CHARTWELL
BOOKS, INC.

A   QUINTET   BOOK

Published by Chartwell Books
A Division of Book Sales, Inc.
110 Enterprise Avenue
Secaucus, New Jersey 07094

This edition produced for sale
in the U.S.A., its territories
and dependencies only.

ISBN 1-55521-923-3

This book was designed and produced by
Quintet Publishing Limited
6 Blundell Street
London N7 9BH

Creative Director: Richard Dewing
Designer: Ian Hunt
Illustrator: Andy Watkins
Project Editor: Katie Preston
Editor: Lydia Darbyshire
Photographer: Chas Wilder

Typeset in Great Britain by
Central Southern Typesetters, Eastbourne
Manufactured in Singapore by Colour Trend
Printed in Singapore by
Star Standard Industries (Pte) Ltd

CONTENTS

~

Introduction

The projects in this book are set out room by room to give you ideas to fill your entire doll's house. Each room has three to four major pieces of furniture and some smaller accessories. The larger pieces are made entirely from wood, and the smaller projects use a range of materials (a full list is given at the beginning of each mini-project).

All the projects have figure diagrams showing the exact measurements of the components of the pieces. These are not drawn full size, but can be enlarged easily.

TOOLS AND EQUIPMENT

The main pieces of wooden furniture can be made with power or hand tools, depending on what equipment you already have, and which you are most familiar with; the step-by-step photographs show the furniture being constructed with the range of power tools listed below. The other pieces of equipment and accessories you will need are also listed.

Accuracy is of prime importance when working on such a small scale. It is therefore important that you constantly check the way the pieces are fitting together: whether all the legs sit squarely to the floor, for example. If you are using power tools, remember to check them regularly: for example, check that all saws are vertical to the machine table; check that your miter gauge is set at 90°.

You will find it useful to make a basic assembly jig, which will help to check that corners are square; you can make one from three pieces of ½ inch plywood glued at right angles to each other (see figure drawing).

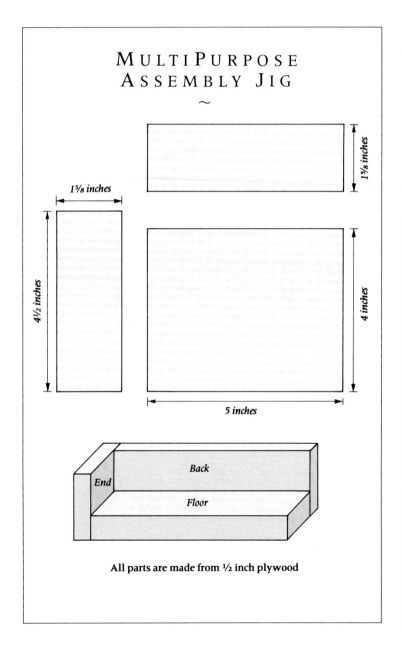

MULTIPURPOSE ASSEMBLY JIG

~

1⅝ inches

1⅝ inches

4½ inches

4 inches

5 inches

Back

End

Floor

All parts are made from ½ inch plywood

HAND TOOLS

~

Claw hammer
Tack hammer
Chisels, Gouges
Screwdrivers, Mat knife
Punch, Hand scroll saw
Handsaws, Pliers
Tweezers, Vise

POWER TOOLS

~

Bandsaw with fence and circle cutting pin, Miter gauge
Power drill and stand with bits
Router and molding bits
Circular saw, Belt sander
Small lathe and tools
Scroll saw
Drum sanders

ACCESSORIES

~

Carpenter's square, Steel ruler
Bulldog clips, Rubber bands
Clamps, Brads
Wooden toothpicks
Metal tapemeasure
Brass knobs, Brass feet
Fine sandpaper

MATERIALS AND TECHNIQUES

Lumber

There are specialist outlets which sell equipment for making doll house furniture, and they will sell small amounts of wood to the thicknesses required for this scale of working. Alternatively, you may find a lumberyard or carpenter who will supply you with cut sections. You will probably find it most useful to obtain pieces about 12 × 5 inches long and wide and from $\frac{1}{8}$ to $\frac{5}{8}$ inch thick. This will give you a choice of sizes that can be sliced to the required size.

The projects use three types of wood, although you may find alternatives. They are:

MAHOGANY Danta – a mahogany-type wood from the Ivory Coast – has been used in some projects. It has a very small and pleasing grain, but has the disadvantage of moving and twisting.

PINE Always make sure you use good-quality pine, since poor-quality pine is difficult to saw and sand.

PLYWOOD Available in a range of thicknesses, from $\frac{1}{16}$ inch upwards. It is often used for the backs of pieces, since this side is not often seen. Plywood does not twist as wood strips are apt to. It is often used as a backing to veneer.

Glues

Always suit the glue to the job at hand.

WOOD GLUE This is the type used most often in the main projects. It is used for gluing wood to wood.

TWO-PART EPOXY RESIN This is used for gluing wood to metal. Use the slow-drying variety, which takes approximately 16 hours to dry. This glue consists of an adhesive and a hardener mixed together; follow the manufacturer's instructions carefully.

MULTIPURPOSE ADHESIVE This clear, yellow, or white household glue is used for gluing fabric, such as chair seats and other upholstery.

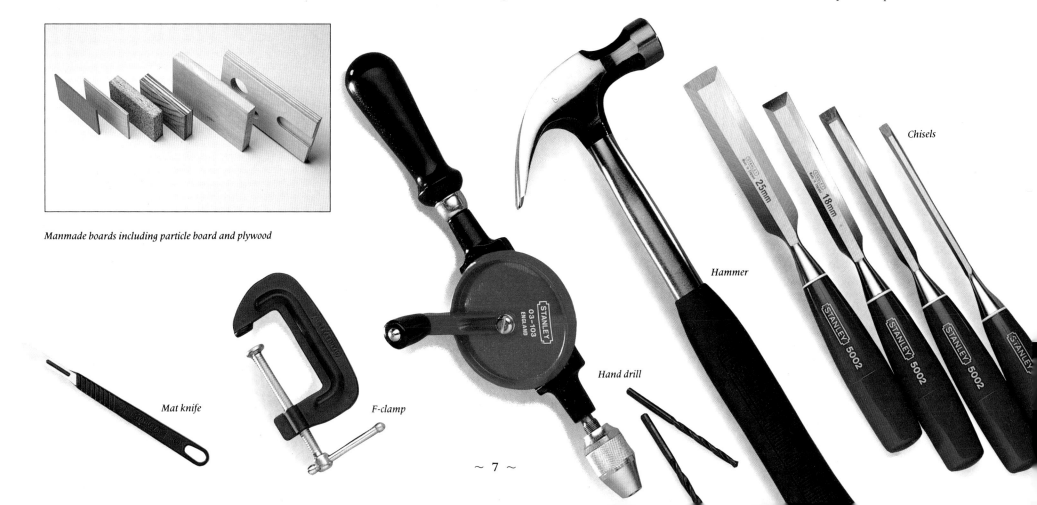

Manmade boards including particle board and plywood

Mat knife

F-clamp

Hand drill

Hammer

Chisels

Finishing

All the instructions indicate when and how each piece should be finished – that is, when it should be sanded, stained, polished and waxed. Where a piece has a large and prominent surface, for example the top, you will have to take a lot of care to finish it properly, applying up to eight coats of polish and leaving to dry overnight.

SANDING It is better to do as much finishing as possible to individual parts before you undertake any assembly. Fine sandpaper is best for cutting and smoothing work. The paper is graded by grit numbers, the lower numbers being coarse, the higher numbers finer. Grade 40 or 60 should be used first for rough-sawn surfaces. Use 100 or 120 grit for a planed or smoother surface, then use 180 or 200 grit. Next use 240 grit, before giving the wood a final sanding with 320 or 360 grit. This plan is for perfectionists, and it can be modified if you wish. You can make or purchase a sanding block around which the paper is wrapped to produce a more even surface. All the dust that is generated must be removed with a cloth or brush before you begin to apply stain or to use any other finishing technique.

STAINING Apply the stain with a rag, although a small brush is useful for getting into difficult corners. Work with the grain. When the work is covered, wipe off any surplus stain with a clean cloth, before leaving the piece to dry overnight. When it is completely dry, the surface may appear to be slightly rough. This will be the result of dust or the stain raising the grain. Use a very fine sandpaper to smooth the surface.

SEALING Sealer is applied for several reasons: it affords some protection to the wood; it slightly hardens the surface; and it prevents the stain from bleeding. You should apply the sealer with a brush or a cotton cloth. The first stroke is made across the grain to lodge the talc filler that is in the sealer into the grain lines. Work quickly because sealer becomes tacky in a very short time. Leave it to dry for 24 hours. If the sealer is absorbed by the wood, apply a second or even a third coat. Sand with a fine-grade paper between coats.

WAXING A paste in which beeswax is the main ingredient is the most suitable. The first application of the wax should be made with a small piece of the finest grade steel wool. Use plenty of wax for this first application and work with the grain. Wipe off any surplus or strands of steel wool with a clean cloth. Leave to harden overnight. The surface can then be polished with a clean, soft cloth.

FINISHING EQUIPMENT

~

Sandpaper in a variety of grades
Dustcloths, Cotton cloths, Stains, Sealer
Steel wool, fine grade
Wax (containing beeswax)
Denatured alcohol, Absorbent cotton, Polish
Burnishing cream

SAFETY

~

Almost all finishing materials and adhesives are toxic. Take great care when you are using or handling them. Work in a well-ventilated room and avoid inhaling either fumes or dust. Store all materials safely and make sure that all waste is disposed of properly. Observe fire precautions at all times, and never smoke in a workshop. Wear protective clothing in case you spill anything. Never store finishers in old food containers and keep them all out of the reach of children.

Fine steel wool

TOP TO BOTTOM: *fine sandpaper, sandpaper, coarse aluminum oxide paper*

FRENCH POLISHING
~

You will need
- ☛ 1 piece of thin cotton rag, approximately 2 × 2 inches
- ☛ Denatured alcohol
- ☛ Absorbent cotton
- ☛ Polish

FORMING THE PAD

1. Soak the cotton rag with denatured alcohol and squeeze out any surplus.

2. Place the rag on a flat surface, add a ball of cotton, and pour on the polish.

3. Turn up the edges of the rag to form a pad.

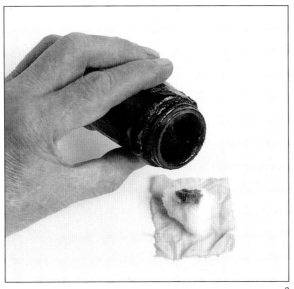

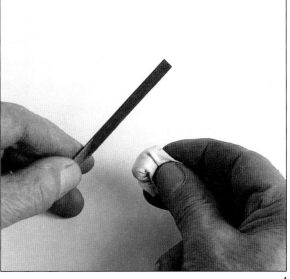

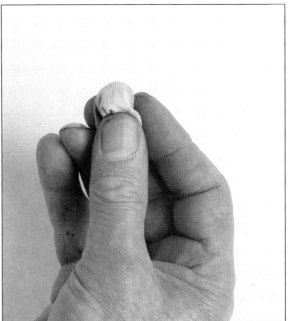

4. Tap the completed pad against a clean surface or the palm of your other hand until the polish appears through the rag. It is very easy to overload a pad with polish. If you do, squeeze out the pad to remove the excess. If the pad is too dry, add more polish. With practice you will learn to put in the correct amount.

POLISHING Stroke the pad along the grain. If you are polishing one piece at a time, allow each coat to dry for three to five minutes before you apply the next. For larger, more visible surfaces apply up to eight coats; five or six coats should be sufficient for smaller surfaces. Allow to dry overnight.

BURNISHING Use a burnishing cream on a piece of rag for the final finish. Apply as for French polish. When it is dry, rub with a soft dustcloth.

Pinning blanks

Between six and eight blanks can be pinned together, depending on their thickness and the length of the drill bit. This will produce several identical shapes from just one cutting process.

The position of the pins will depend on the piece being made – under the seat between the legs for chairs, for example. The length of the pin should be such that, when it is driven into the block, the heads are flush with the top of the block, but the pointed ends protrude by approximately $1/16$ inch at the bottom.

Place the assembly jig on the drill table. Adjust the depth of drilling to $1/16$ inch from the jig floor. This will fasten the bottom blank more firmly and stop it from falling off. Place the blanks on the jig and drill both pin holes. Hold the blanks together with your fingers and drive the pins into the holes with a heavy hammer. Sand the pin tips so that they are flush.

Drill a hole through the blanks for the pin.

Drive the pin into the block until the head is flush with the top.

GLOSSARY OF TERMS

BIAS-CUT Cutting across the grain.

CARCASS The basic framework of a piece.

CHAMFER A narrow, flat surface angled at 45°, planed or carved on the edge of a section.

COLUMN The decorative part of the leg, attached to the underside of the table, which is molded and shaped.

COVER SLIP A small, thin strip of wood that covers the rough front edge of a slice of wood.

GROOVE A long, narrow channel cut into the wood. Grooves act mainly as shelf bearers.

JIG A guide to accuracy used in assembly to hold the correct angles while the glue sets, and also as a guide when sawing.

LATERAL The pieces of the *carcass* that fit horizontally.

LEG HOLDER The second component of a complex leg construction. It is a small, round section of wood with three slits cut at 120° to each other, into which the legs fit.

LIPPED DRAWER A drawer which has an additional front piece which overlaps the drawer front beneath by approximately $1/16$ inch.

MIDDLE UPRIGHT The pieces of the *carcass* that fit vertically.

MITER A corner joint formed between two pieces of material, for example wood, by cutting the ends at equal angles, for example two angles of 45° joining to make a right angle of 90°.

RABBET A step cut along the edge of a piece of wood into which another piece of wood fits – often used to hold the back of a piece.

SPLAT A piece of wood that forms the horizontal central part of a chair back. The splat may be plain or a decorative feature.

STOP A small square of wood which fits into a groove to prevent a shelf, for example, from moving in the groove.

UPSTANDS The decorative edging on the top of the desk that consists of three strips of wood fitted into grooves in the top.

VENEER A thin layer of wood with a decorative or fine finish that is bonded to the surface of a less expensive material such as plywood.

THE KITCHEN

~

Kitchen Table

~

This lovely pine table is a perfect centerpiece in any kitchen. Choose a good piece of pine with a pretty grain for the top, since this element will be the most visible. The construction is relatively simple, but the detailing – such as the mitered edging and the shaped legs – makes the piece very special.

~

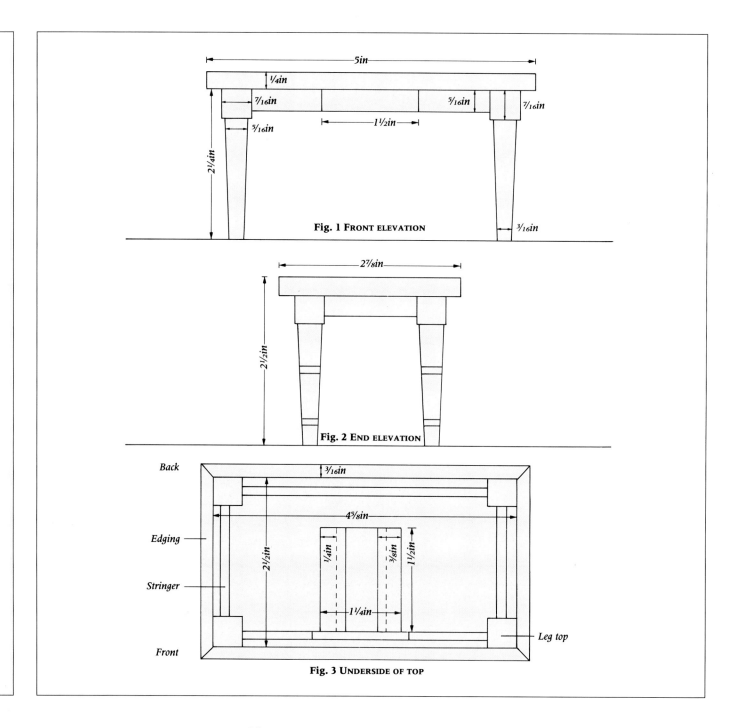

Fig. 1 FRONT ELEVATION

Fig. 2 END ELEVATION

Fig. 3 UNDERSIDE OF TOP

MAKING THE TOP
~

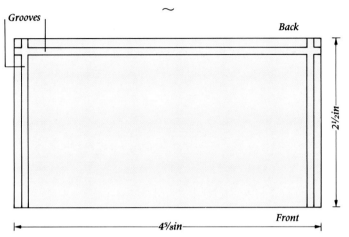

Fig. 4 UNDERSIDE OF TOP TO SHOW GROOVES

1. Cut a piece of pine for the table top 4⅝ × 2½ × ¼ inches. Make grooves for the back and end stringers ⅛ inch wide and deep and ⅛ inch from the edges.

2. For the edging, cut a section 2 × ³⁄₁₆ × 5⅜ inches. You will need a 5⅝ inch strip for the back and two end strips 3¼ inch long. Miter the ends of the edging strips to 45°, testing for fit against the table top. Glue the strips to the table top. Hand sand or belt sand the table surface.

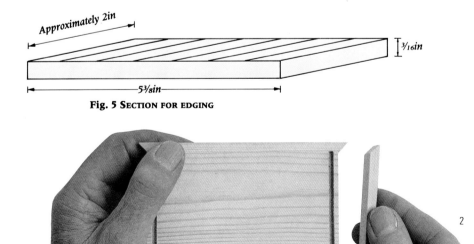

Fig. 5 SECTION FOR EDGING

MAKING THE LEGS
~

Fig. 6a LEGS

Fig. 6b

Fig. 6c

Fig. 6d

Cut heads to ⁷⁄₁₆in

3. Cut two square blanks for the legs. Each blank will make two legs – the center of the blank is the foot. Shape the blank in the sequence illustrated: turn the blank until it is ⁵⁄₁₆ inch in diameter; turn the foot until it is ³⁄₁₆ inch, cut it at a slight taper to match with the total taper; taper the legs and sand; run the rings. Sand the square heads. Dust, wax and polish.

4. Cut the leg heads to ⁷⁄₁₆ inch, making sure that all the leg heads are exactly the same height. Make the final cut to the legs to give a total length of 2¼ inches. Sand the end of the legs and heads with fine sandpaper.

5. For the back and end stringers, cut a piece of pine $\frac{7}{16} \times 4\frac{1}{4} \times \frac{1}{8}$ inches long. Check the fit across the width of the groove. Sand, dust and wax one side of all the strips. Measure each piece against the underside of the table, with the legs in place, and then cut to fit.

6. For the front stringer run a section $\frac{3}{8} \times 4\frac{1}{4}$ inches. The front stringer, which is initially glued to the drawer front, will have two cuts made in it to free the drawer front, and it needs to be cut slightly longer than the back stringer to compensate for this. Make two cuts to the drawer front strip and check that the three joined pieces exactly match the back stringer.

7. Choose the two best legs for the front of the table. Apply glue to one back leg and to the table top and glue in place. Put glue into the back groove and insert the stringer, checking for upright. Glue the second back leg. Glue the end stringers and front legs in the same way.

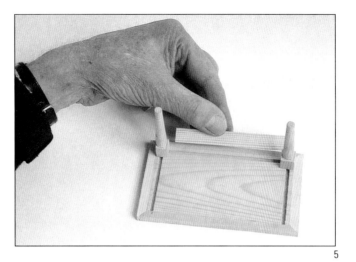

5

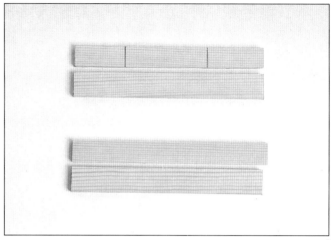

6

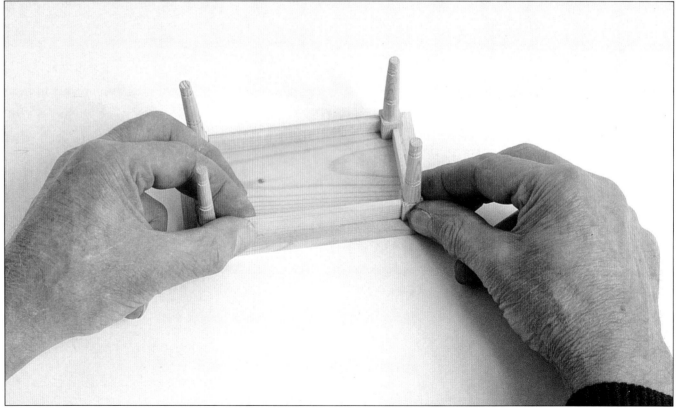

7

8. Cut the drawer bottom ¹⁄₁₆ inch thick. Cut a section (see Fig. 5 as for edging) and slice strips ¹⁄₄ × 1 ¹⁄₂ inches for the drawer sides. Glue the sides to the bottom and leave to dry.

Glue the front stringer to the drawer front, matching the center of the drawer to a center mark on the stringer.

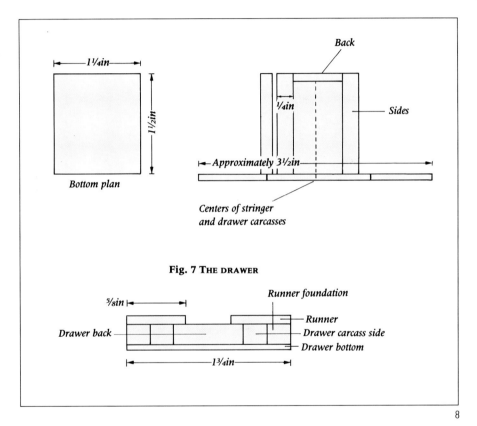

Fig. 7 THE DRAWER

10

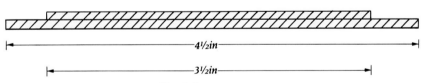

Fig. 8 ASSEMBLY JIG

9. Separate the drawer front from the rest of the stringer. The ends should protrude ¹⁄₈ inch from the drawer sides. Cut and fit the drawer back (Fig. 7).

9

10. Make the assembly jig (see Fig. 8). Position the drawer and front stringer and push the assembly jig against pieces. Make sure that the gaps between the ends of the drawer front and the stringers are the same. Cut a section for the drawer runner foundations (as Fig. 5), but add the height of the drawer bottom to the thickness of the piece. Slice two foundation strips ¹⁄₄ inch wide. Cut the strips 1 ¹⁄₂ inches long. Glue the foundations to the drawer. When the glue is dry, glue the side parts of the front stringer to the table top.

11. Make the drawer runners by cutting two strips ⅝ × ¹⁄₁₆ × 1½ inches. Glue the strips to the runner foundations. Make sure the glue does not jam the drawer. Drill a hole in the drawer front for a brass knob ⅛ inch in diameter.

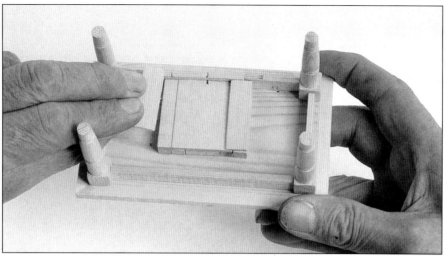

11

Alternative Method
~

You can make this table without the grooves. Proceed in the same way, but make the stringers ⁵⁄₁₆ inch high. Instead of placing the back and end stringers in grooves, they will have to be assembled using using the jig as described for the front stringers and drawer front. Make a smaller jig in the same way for the end stringers, or assemble them by eye.

Kitchen Bench

~

A lovely accompaniment to the kitchen table (page 12), this bench, also made in pine, uses some of the same design features, such as the mitered edging. The legs are made by constructing an A-frame and slicing cross-sections from the frame. This means the leg pieces are exactly the same height and shape, and it also makes it easier to create more than one bench at a time.

~

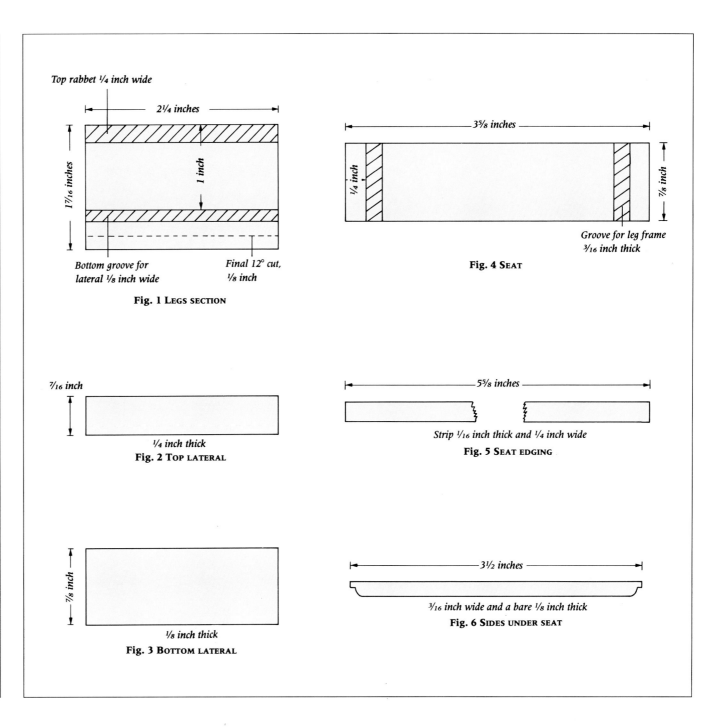

Top rabbet ¼ inch wide

2¼ inches

1⁷⁄₁₆ inches

1 inch

Bottom groove for lateral ⅛ inch wide

Final 12° cut, ⅛ inch

Fig. 1 LEGS SECTION

3⅝ inches

¼ inch

⅞ inch

Groove for leg frame ³⁄₁₆ inch thick

Fig. 4 SEAT

⁷⁄₁₆ inch

¼ inch thick
Fig. 2 TOP LATERAL

5⅝ inches

Strip ¹⁄₁₆ inch thick and ¼ inch wide
Fig. 5 SEAT EDGING

⅞ inch

⅛ inch thick
Fig. 3 BOTTOM LATERAL

3½ inches

³⁄₁₆ inch wide and a bare ⅛ inch thick
Fig. 6 SIDES UNDER SEAT

1

3

1. Bias-cut a section 1⁷⁄₁₆ × 1 × 1 inches. From this section cut two strips ⅛ inch thick across the grain. Cut a ⅛ inch groove 1 inch from the edge and at a 12° angle. Cut a ¼ inch wide rabbet, also at a 12° angle, along the opposite side of the strips. Make the final cut (see Fig. 1) at a 12° angle.

2. Cut the two lateral pieces (see Figs. 2 and 3).

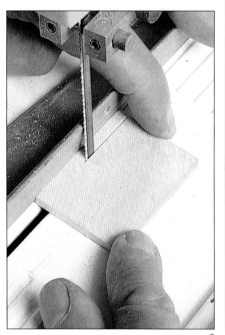

2

4

3. Put glue in the grooves and rabbets on the leg slices. Insert the bottom and then the top lateral. Wait for the glue to dry.

4. Slice the leg frames as cross-sections ³⁄₁₆ inch thick.

5. Cut the bench seat (see Fig. 4). Cut ³/₁₆ inch-wide grooves in the underside to take the leg frames. Cut two seat edging strips (see Fig. 5). Miter and glue the edgings to the seat.

6. Glue the leg frames into the grooves in the seat.

7. Cut two strips and mold them to the shape shown in Fig. 6. Glue these strips to the underside of the bench. Sand and wax the top surface and edges of the seat, the leg frame, and one side of the bench sides.

5

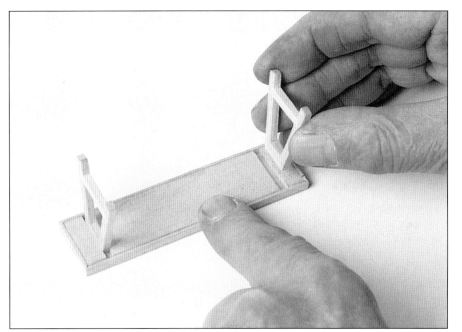

6

7

Pine Corner Cabinet

~

The clever construction of this cabinet – slicing the shelves from a triangular block – will mean that all the shelves are exactly the same size, that the back pieces fit properly, and that the cabinet will fit into the corner snugly. The molded pieces at the top and bottom, and the shaped shelf fronts, add a decorative touch.

~

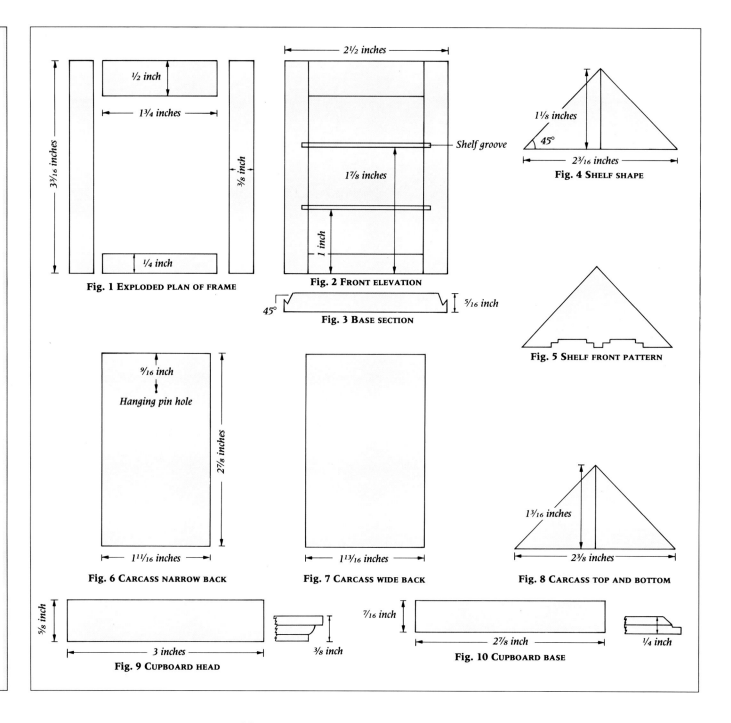

Fig. 1 EXPLODED PLAN OF FRAME

½ inch

1¾ inches

3³⁄₁₆ inches

⅜ inch

¼ inch

2½ inches

Shelf groove

1⅞ inches

1 inch

Fig. 2 FRONT ELEVATION

45°   ⁵⁄₁₆ inch

Fig. 3 BASE SECTION

1⅛ inches

45°

2³⁄₁₆ inches

Fig. 4 SHELF SHAPE

Fig. 5 SHELF FRONT PATTERN

⁹⁄₁₆ inch

Hanging pin hole

2⅞ inches

1¹¹⁄₁₆ inches

Fig. 6 CARCASS NARROW BACK

1¹³⁄₁₆ inches

Fig. 7 CARCASS WIDE BACK

1³⁄₁₆ inches

2⅜ inches

Fig. 8 CARCASS TOP AND BOTTOM

⅝ inch

3 inches   ⅜ inch

Fig. 9 CUPBOARD HEAD

⁷⁄₁₆ inch

2⅞ inch   ¼ inch

Fig. 10 CUPBOARD BASE

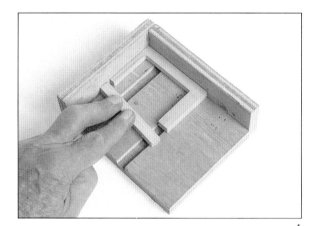

1. Cut the components of the basic frame 5/16 inch thick (see Fig. 1). Assemble and glue the frame together.

2. Cut the base section, as shown in Fig. 3, to a 45° angle. Cut two 1/8 inch grooves in the frame for the shelves. Sand and wax the front and side edges.

4. Shape the front of the triangular block as shown in Fig. 5.

5. Slice shelves from the block to the width of the shelf grooves already cut. Assemble the shelves in the carcass.

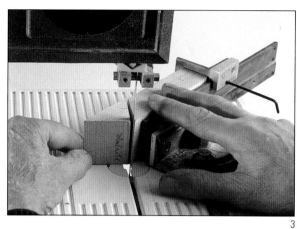

3. Cut a section 1½ × ¾ × 6 inches along the grain. Cut a triangular block from this section to make the shelves (see Fig. 4). Keep any remaining pieces to form the top and bottom of the carcass.

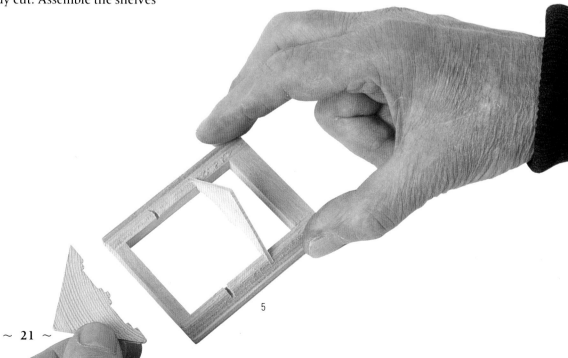

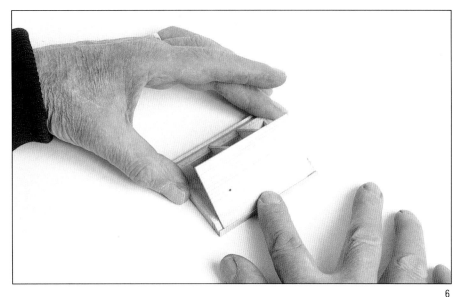

6. Cut pieces for the carcass back ¹⁄₁₆ inch thick. Drill the hanging holes in the narrower piece. (see Figs. 6 and 7.) Fit the narrow piece first.

7. Use a rubber band to hold the back pieces in place.

8. Cut the top and bottom pieces (Fig. 8) from the block made in step 3. Fit and glue the base and top in position.

9. Cut blanks for the cupboard head and base. Mold the fronts and ends. (see Figs. 9 and 10.)

10. Make a 45° cut to the corners of the base and head pieces. This cut will be ³⁄₁₆ inch from the front edge of these pieces. Sand and wax the base and heads.

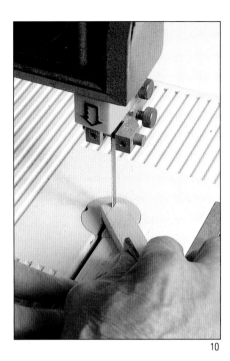

10

11. Glue the base and head in place. Cut a pad ½ inch square and ¼ inch deep, and glue it to the underside of the carcass.

11

Note
~

Each time you make this cabinet, it will have slightly different measurements. The measurements in Fig. 2 form the basis for all subsequent measurements; all pieces made after the basic frame should be measured against the frame and cut to fit; the measurements given are approximate.

Pine Hanging Shelves

~

A decorative but useful piece for any kitchen, these shelves work best in pine, since the light color and simple designs complement the bright colors used in many kitchens. The small drawers beneath the bottom shelf are constructed in exactly the same way as the drawers in the other projects.

~

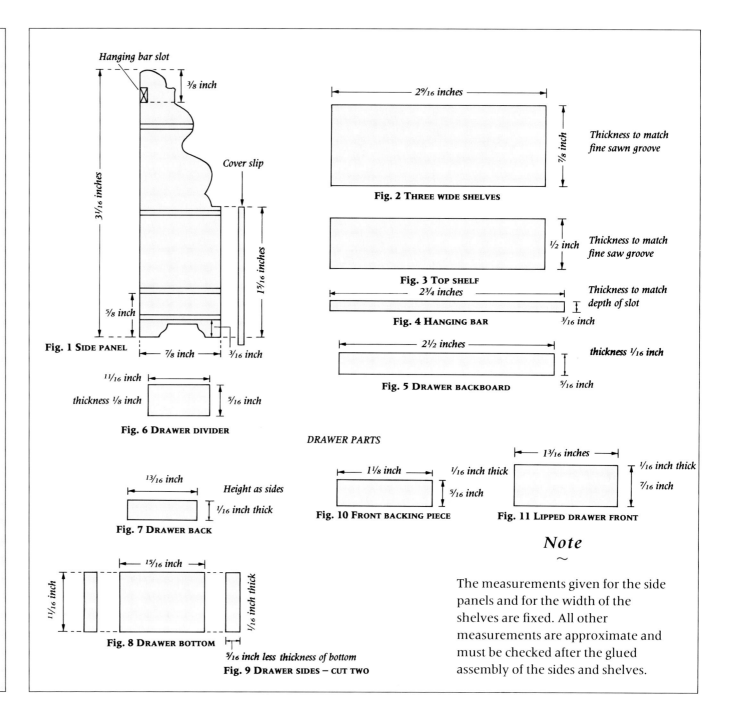

Hanging bar slot

³/₈ inch

Cover slip

3¹/₁₆ inches

1⁵/₁₆ inches

⁵/₈ inch

Fig. 1 SIDE PANEL

⁷/₈ inch   ³/₁₆ inch

2⁹/₁₆ inches

⁷/₈ inch

Thickness to match fine sawn groove

Fig. 2 THREE WIDE SHELVES

½ inch

Thickness to match fine saw groove

Fig. 3 TOP SHELF

2¾ inches

Thickness to match depth of slot

³/₁₆ inch

Fig. 4 HANGING BAR

2½ inches

thickness ¹/₁₆ inch

⁵/₁₆ inch

Fig. 5 DRAWER BACKBOARD

¹¹/₁₆ inch

thickness ⅛ inch

⁵/₁₆ inch

Fig. 6 DRAWER DIVIDER

DRAWER PARTS

1⅛ inch

¹/₁₆ inch thick

⁵/₁₆ inch

Fig. 10 FRONT BACKING PIECE

1³/₁₆ inches

¹/₁₆ inch thick

⁷/₁₆ inch

Fig. 11 LIPPED DRAWER FRONT

1³/₁₆ inch

Height as sides

¹/₁₆ inch thick

Fig. 7 DRAWER BACK

1⁵/₁₆ inch

1¹/₁₆ inch

¹/₁₆ inch thick

Fig. 8 DRAWER BOTTOM

⁵/₁₆ inch less thickness of bottom

Fig. 9 DRAWER SIDES – CUT TWO

Note

~

The measurements given for the side panels and for the width of the shelves are fixed. All other measurements are approximate and must be checked after the glued assembly of the sides and shelves.

1

2

3

4

1. You will need a section ⅞ inch wide and 3³⁄₁₆ inches long and sufficiently deep to provide slices for the sides, the shelves and the cover slips. Cut generous 3¹⁄₁₆ × ⅞ × ¹⁄₁₆ inches slices for the side pieces. Make grooves to the measurements shown in Fig. 1.

2. Draw the pattern onto the sides. If you are cutting more than one set of sides, you can pin several slices together and cut all the sides in one go (see *pinning blanks*). Cut the hanging bar slot in the sides.

3. Make the molded cuts for the feet.

4. Cut out the pattern.

5. Slice two cover slips from the blank already made and cut them to 1⁵/₁₆ inches long. Glue the cover strips to the sides. They should be flush with the top edge of the front and protrude by ⅛ inch at the bottom, where they are trimmed off with a mat knife.

6. The unpinned block, showing the sides with pattern and grooves cut.

7. For the shelves, cut four slices from the section made in step 1. Reduce the width of one slice to match the depth of the top shelf groove. Cut all the shelves to a finished length of 2⁹/₁₆ inches (see Figs. 2 and 3). Sand and wax the visible surfaces. Glue the shelves to the side panels on the jig.

8. Cut the drawer backboard (see Fig. 5) and test for fit against the carcass. Sand and wax.

9. Cut the drawer divider (see Fig. 6) and test for fit. Sand and wax.

10. Cut the hanging bar (see Fig. 4) and make the holes marked, test for fit, and then sand and wax it. Make sure the ends of the hanging bar are flush with the sides.

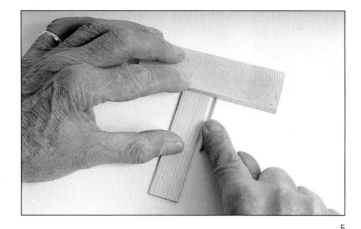

5

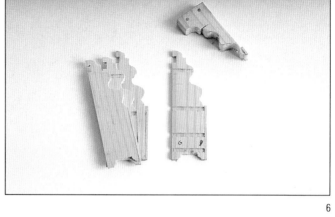

6

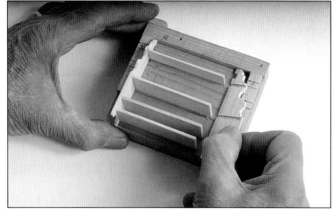

7

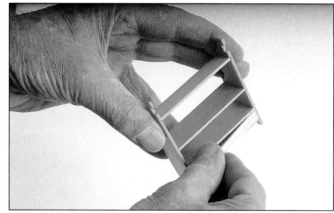

8

9

10

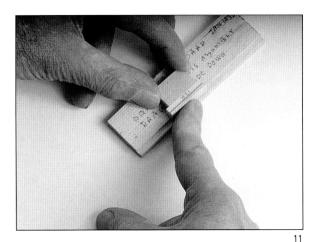

11

11. Cut, sand and wax the drawer components (see Figs. 7–11). Apply glue to the front edge of the bottom piece and glue to the front piece. Apply glue to the front and bottom of the right side. Leave glue to set and then assemble the left side in the same way. Test for fit against the assembled carcass. The lipped drawer front should overlap the top, bottom and sides by about ¹⁄₁₆ inch.

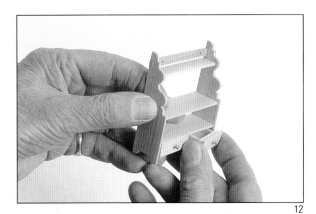

12

12. Make small holes in the drawer fronts for the knobs, apply glue and insert. Place the carcass on its back and leave to dry overnight.

Mantel Clock

~

This is a replica of a German dollhouse clock dating from the 1840s.

You Will Need

~

- ☞ Hardwood for clock body 1 × ⅝ × ⅝ inches; for base 1 × ⅝ × ⅛ inches; for pediment 1 × ⅝ × ⅜ inches; for feet, 4 pieces, each ¼ × ¼ × ⅛ inches
- ☞ Fine sandpaper
- ☞ Flat-finish enamel paint (black) or mahogany wood stain and French polish
- ☞ Thin bone knitting needle or ivory-painted toothpick, cut into 4 pieces, each ⅝ inch
- ☞ Large, flat-headed thumbtack
- ☞ Small paper printed clock face (draw or photocopy the example shown here)
- ☞ Clear varnish
- ☞ Wood glue
- ☞ Superglue gel
- ☞ Gloss enamel paint (ivory), if needed for pillars.

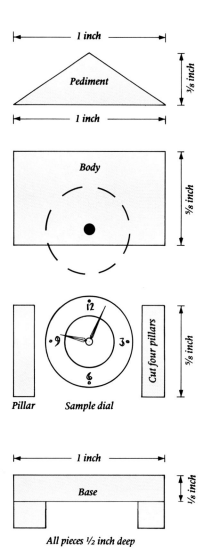

All pieces ½ inch deep

1. Cut out the pieces of wood. Smooth all surfaces with fine sandpaper and finish all visible surfaces with either mahogany wood stain and French polish to imitate the rosewood antique version or with flat black enamel paint.

2. Glue the pediment to the clock body. Back the clock face with thin cardboard and glue it to the head of the thumbtack. Varnish it. Drill a hole in the clock body with a fine spiral drill. Put some glue on the shank of the pin and push it firmly into the hole. Using a drill will prevent the wood from splitting.

3. Glue the feet to the clock base. Set the pillars at each corner of the base, press each one firmly in a dab of glue onto the base and allow to set. Apply a spot of glue to the tops of the pillar and stand the clock body in place on the pillars, making sure that the body and base are aligned. Press firmly in place and leave to dry.

~

Bed

~

This design is one of the simplest in terms of the number of components. However, you will still need to work as carefully and accurately as possible. As with any piece with separate legs, you will have to be especially careful to make sure all the legs are level. You could shape the headboard to any design you wish – perhaps a simple rounded shape.

~

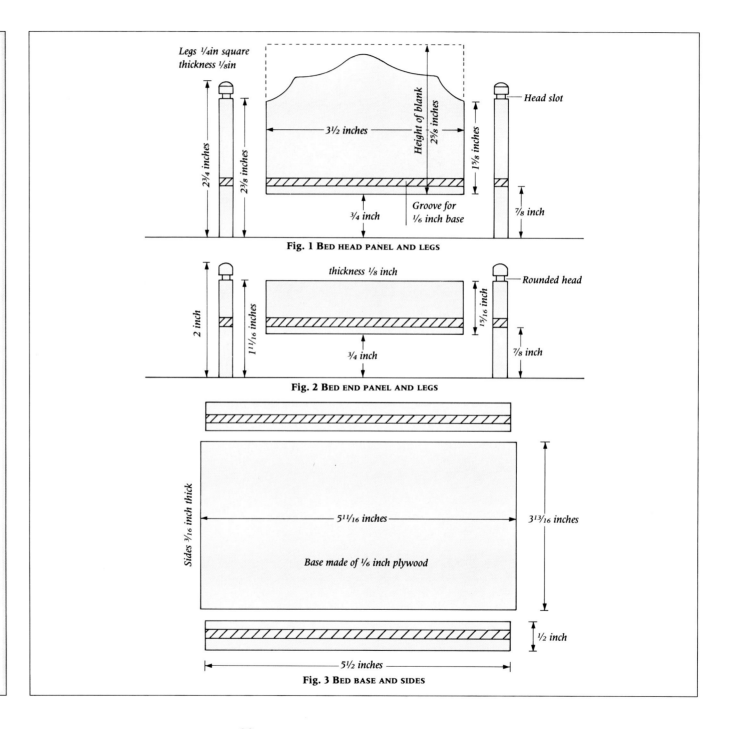

Fig. 1 BED HEAD PANEL AND LEGS

Fig. 2 BED END PANEL AND LEGS

Fig. 3 BED BASE AND SIDES

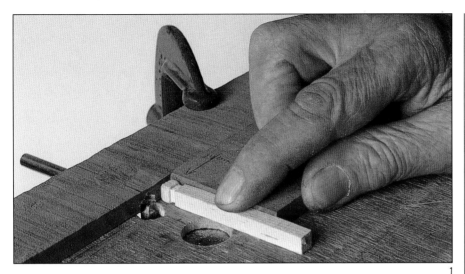

1. Cut out four pine legs. Make slots in the heads and round the tops (see Fig. 1).

2. Take a piece of pine to the dimensions shown in Fig. 1 for the headboard. Make a line down the middle and draw in the headboard shape, making sure the pattern is exactly symmetrical around the center line. Cut the headboard out.

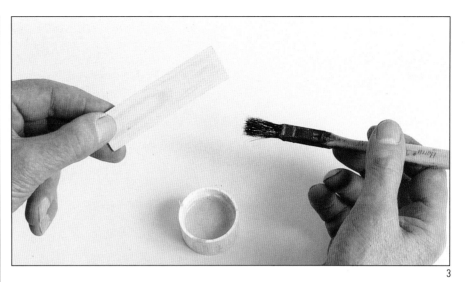

3. Cut out the end panel (see Fig. 2). Sand, seal and wax both panels.

4. Assemble the legs and the headboard by butting them together and gluing. The top edge of each panel should be slightly below the bottom edge of the leg head slots. Allow the glue to set. Repeat for the legs and the end panel.

5. Cut ⅙ inch base grooves in both the assembled panels.

7. Dry-assemble the base to the head and end panels. Measure the distance between the head legs and end legs. Cut the base side pieces (see Fig. 3) so that they are very slightly longer than this measurement. Cut a ⅙ inch groove in each side.

8. Sand, seal and wax the sides. Use a toothpick to put glue in the side grooves and position the sides to the base so that the base protrudes equally on both sides.

6. Make some "stops" to fill the grooves and keep the base board from moving. They need to be the depth of the groove and a bare ³⁄₁₆ inch long. Glue the stops no more than ⅛ inch into the groove and running with the grain. Test the distance between the stops with a ruler – they must be at least 3¹³⁄₁₆ inches apart for the base to fit easily. Sand the stops so they are flush with the leg surface. Sand, seal and wax the legs.

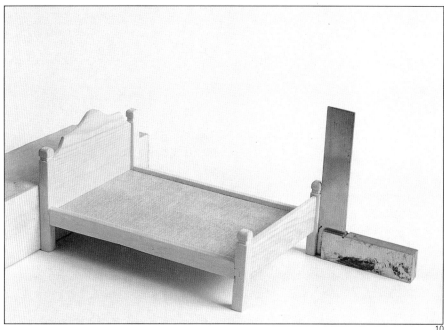

9. Assemble the base to the head and glue in position.

10. Assemble the end to the base and glue in position. Leave to dry, making sure that all four legs are square to a flat surface.

Bedside Table

~

This simple but charming design is an essential piece in any bedroom, and it complements the pine bed (see page 30) perfectly. The feet are shaped by cutting out semi and quarter circles, as are the lateral pieces beneath the table top. The legs are made of lengths of dowel.

~

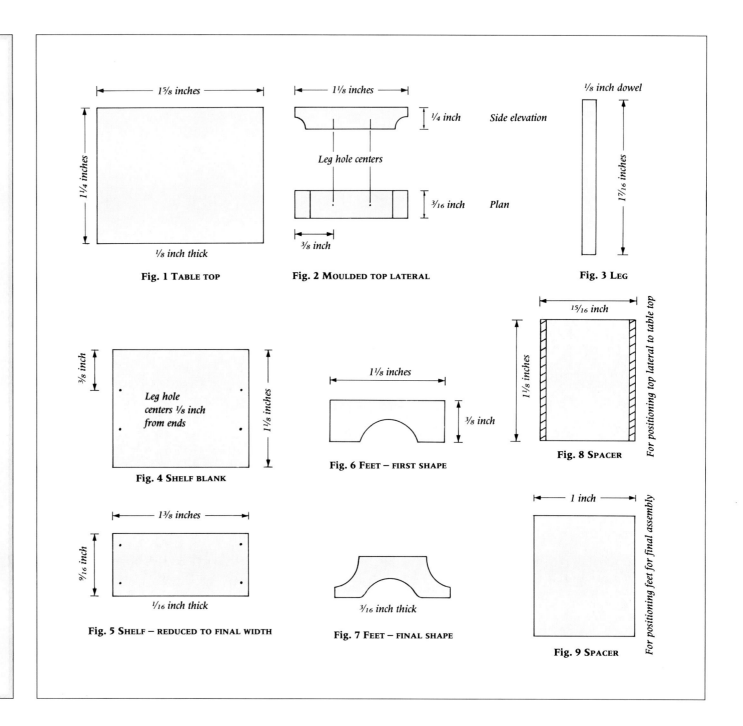

Fig. 1 TABLE TOP

Fig. 2 MOULDED TOP LATERAL

Fig. 3 LEG

Fig. 4 SHELF BLANK

Fig. 6 FEET – FIRST SHAPE

Fig. 8 SPACER

Fig. 5 SHELF – REDUCED TO FINAL WIDTH

Fig. 7 FEET – FINAL SHAPE

Fig. 9 SPACER

1. All the pieces shown are cut from pine except the two spacers (Figs. 8 and 9), which are cut from scrap wood. For the feet, cut two blanks $1\frac{1}{8} \times \frac{3}{8} \times \frac{3}{16}$ inches. To shape the feet, first hollow out the center semicircle.

2. Hollow out two quarter-circles from each side to form the final shape of the feet.

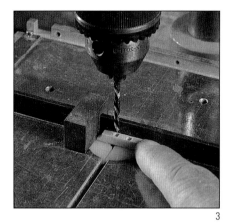

3. Cut two top lateral pieces $1\frac{1}{8} \times \frac{1}{4}$ inches and $\frac{3}{16}$ inch wide, and mold to the shape shown (see Fig. 2). These pieces sit underneath the table top at the top of the legs. Drill two holes for the legs, each $\frac{3}{8}$ inch from the end of the lateral.

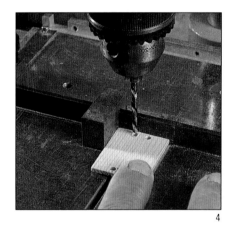

4. To make the shelf, cut a section $1\frac{1}{8}$ inch wide and at least 2 inches long. Cut along the grain so that it is barely $\frac{1}{8}$ inch thick. Trim the section down so that it is $1\frac{3}{8}$ inches long. Make four leg holes $\frac{3}{8}$ inch from the edge as shown in Fig. 4.

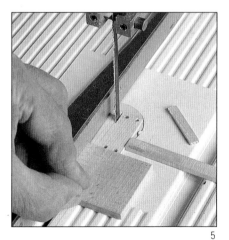

5. Reduce the width of the shelf to $\frac{9}{16}$ inch, which is the length of the flat surface of the feet pieces minus $\frac{1}{16}$ inch. You may have to do this by a process of trial and error. The holes in the shelf must be equidistant from both sides.

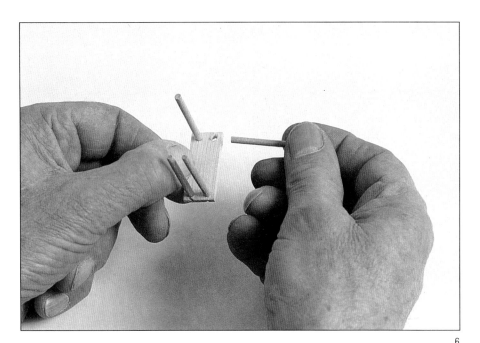

6

8. Put some glue on the underside of the table top and attach it, using the spacer to ensure accuracy. Put some glue on the top, flat surface of the feet and glue them to the shelf so that the feet pieces are in line with the shelf ends and the shelf is centered over the feet pieces. Use the 1 inch-wide spacer to position the feet in the final assembly.

8

6. Cut the top piece (Fig. 1). Hand sand and wax the top surfaces and edges of the table top and shelf, the legs, the outside surface and molding of the top lateral, and the side surfaces and shaping of the feet

pieces. Take four pieces of ⅛ inch dowel (Fig. 3), insert some glue into the holes in the shelf and push in the legs. Check that the ends are flush with the underside of the shelf.

7. Cut the wide spacer and make "anti-glue" rabbets down each side, as shown in Fig. 8. Place the table top upside-down on an assembly jig. Place the spacer on top. Put glue in the holes in the laterals and insert the legs. Check that the shelf is in line with the table top edge. Remove the table top. Check the shelf is parallel to the jig floor; check the legs are vertical from the end and the front. Allow the glued legs to dry.

7

Chest of Drawers

~

This piece is made of mahogany-style wood, but could just as easily be made from pine, depending on your decoration scheme. The feet are not separate components, but are simply formed by shaping the bottom edge of the sides and the front apron. All the visible surfaces – the back is made of plywood – will need to be finished thoroughly, using several coats of polish.

~

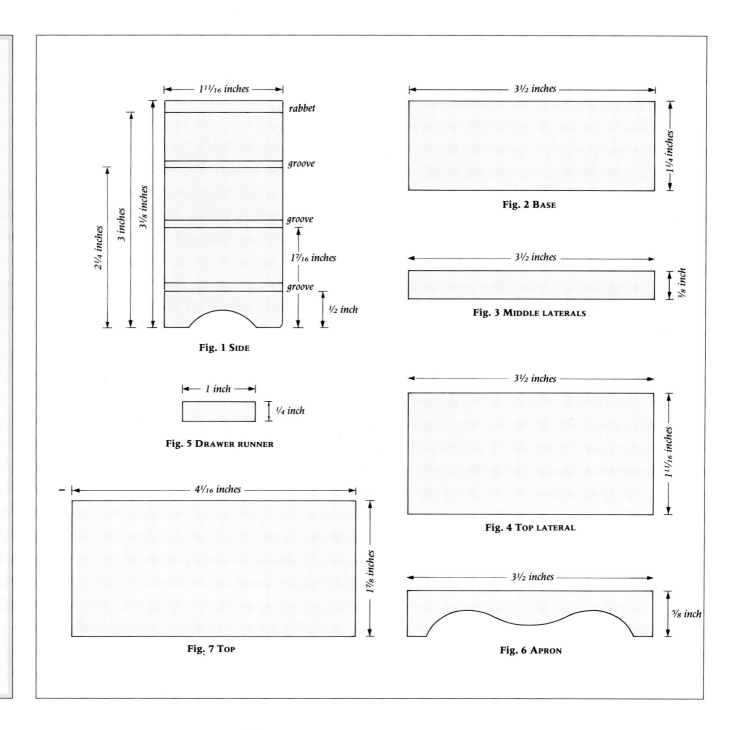

Fig. 1 Side

Fig. 2 Base

Fig. 3 Middle laterals

Fig. 5 Drawer runner

Fig. 4 Top lateral

Fig. 7 Top

Fig. 6 Apron

1. You will need a section of wood 2 × 3¾ × 1¾ inches. From this you can cut two sides, one top lateral, two middle laterals, one base, and four drawer runners. For the sides, cut off two slices to the dimensions shown in Fig. 1. Cut three grooves about ⅛ inch wide for the middle laterals and one rabbet ⅛ inch wide for the top lateral. Cut a rabbet down each side to hold the back.

2. To form the feet, cut out a semi-circle as shown in Fig. 1. Measure the depth of the grooves and rabbet. Cut out the base, one top lateral, two middle laterals, and four drawer runners (Figs. 2–5), making the width match the depth of the grooves and rabbet. Cut the back (Fig. 8) from ⅙ inch plywood and test for fit against the side rabbet.

3. Make plugs for the front ends of the grooves cut for the base. Cut pieces to the depth of the groove and about ³⁄₁₆ inch long. Glue the stops to the grooves so that they protrude slightly at the front. Hand sand the inner and front sides so that the plugs are flush. Sand, stain, and polish the front edges and sides, and the middle and top laterals.

1

2

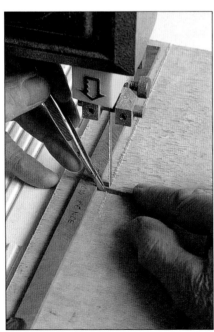

3

4. Assemble the drawer runners. Position the back end of the runners flush with the rabbet for the back. Put glue in the grooves and insert the runners, using a small piece of wood to check that they are vertical.

4

5. Assemble the carcass. Put glue in the grooves and rabbets on the sides. Place the left side on an assembly jig with the feet pressed against the jig wall. Assemble the back so that its top matches the top of the side.

6. Assemble the base flush to the rabbet wall. Assemble the right side and the top lateral.

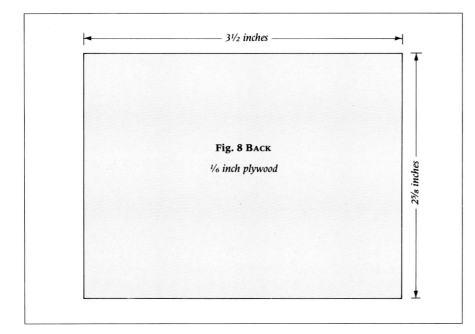

— 3½ inches —

Fig. 8 Back

⅙ inch plywood

2⅝ inches

7. Assemble the middle laterals and the ends, which should be flush with the front edges of the sides.

8. Cut a section ⅝ inch wide along the grain and ½ × 3⅝ inches. Measure the distance between the sides of the assembled carcass to determine the width of the apron. Cut out the apron to the shape shown in Fig. 6. If you want to ensure a snug fit, cut out the apron in ⅙ inch plywood and test it for fit.

9. Sand, stain and polish the front of the apron. Slice the section so that it is slightly less thick than the distance between the front edges of the sides and base. Fit the apron.

8

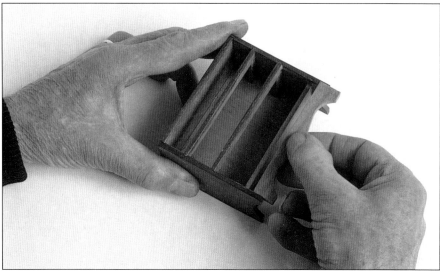

9

MAKING A SET OF DRAWERS

~

Fig. 9 DRAWERS

Sides

Sides

7/16 inch back · Bottom · 9/16 inch backing piece · 11/16 inch lipped front

TOP DRAWER

9/16 inch back · Bottom · 11/16 inch backing piece · 13/16 inch lipped front

MIDDLE DRAWER

Back · 3/4 inch backing piece · 15/16 inch lipped front

BOTTOM DRAWER

All the bottom and side pieces of the drawer are the same depth – 1⁵/₁₆ inch; all the backing pieces are the same width – 3⁷/₁₆ inches; and all the lipped fronts are the same width – 3⁹/₁₆ inches.

Assemble the drawers by placing the drawer front backing piece against the vertical back of a basic assembly jig. Apply glue to the front of the drawer bottom and to the backing piece. Apply glue to the front and the bottom of the right-hand side as you look at it. Holding a small square of wood in your right hand, press it against the edge of the drawer bottom and side so that they line up exactly. Push the side against the backing piece. Allow the glue to set. Assemble the left-hand side. Fit the back. Fit the lipped drawer front, which should overlap the drawer opening top, bottom and sides by about ¹/₁₆ inch. Sand, stain, and polish the drawer fronts and leave to dry overnight.

10

10. Mark where the knobs will go – about ¾ inch from the edge. Make the holes, apply some glue to the knobs and insert. Remove the drawers. Sand, stain, and polish the carcass sides. Cut the top (Fig. 4) and glue it to the carcass. Sand, stain and polish the top. Leave to dry overnight.

Dresser

~

This is one of three carcasses similar in their basic structure; the others are the desk and the sideboard. The structure of the drawers and of course the number of grooves and rabbets required to hold the drawers differ, but once you have mastered one design, you will be able to complete the other two without difficulty.

~

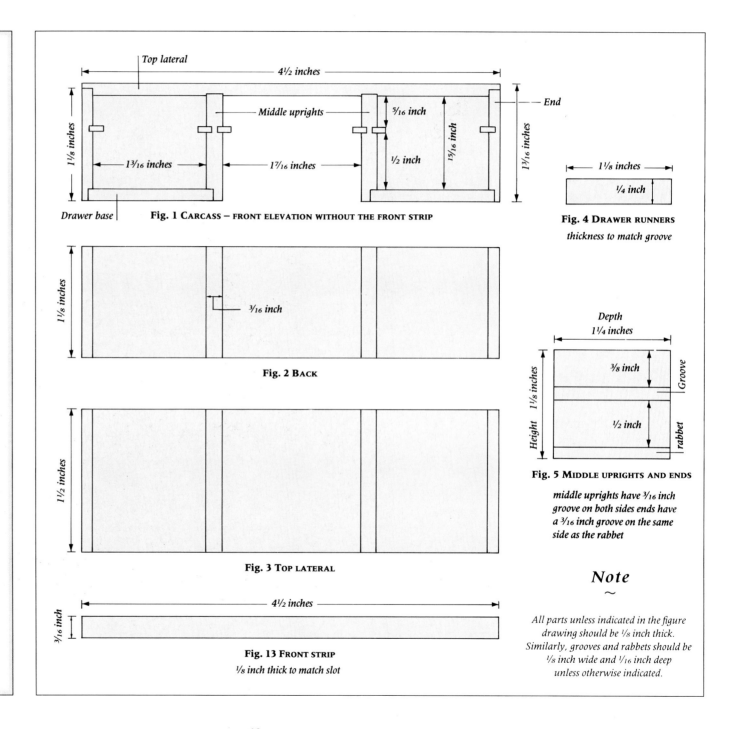

Fig. 1 CARCASS – FRONT ELEVATION WITHOUT THE FRONT STRIP

Top lateral

End

Middle uprights

Drawer base

$4\frac{1}{2}$ inches

$1\frac{1}{8}$ inches

$1\frac{3}{16}$ inches

$1\frac{7}{16}$ inches

$\frac{5}{16}$ inch

$\frac{1}{2}$ inch

$\frac{15}{16}$ inch

$1\frac{3}{16}$ inches

Fig. 2 BACK

$1\frac{1}{8}$ inches

$\frac{3}{16}$ inch

Fig. 3 TOP LATERAL

$1\frac{1}{2}$ inches

Fig. 4 DRAWER RUNNERS

thickness to match groove

$1\frac{1}{8}$ inches

$\frac{1}{4}$ inch

Fig. 5 MIDDLE UPRIGHTS AND ENDS

Depth $1\frac{1}{4}$ inches

Height $1\frac{1}{8}$ inches

$\frac{3}{8}$ inch

$\frac{1}{2}$ inch

Groove

rabbet

middle uprights have $\frac{3}{16}$ inch groove on both sides ends have a $\frac{3}{16}$ inch groove on the same side as the rabbet

Fig. 13 FRONT STRIP

$\frac{1}{8}$ inch thick to match slot

$4\frac{1}{2}$ inches

$\frac{3}{16}$ inch

Note

~

All parts unless indicated in the figure drawing should be $\frac{1}{8}$ inch thick. Similarly, grooves and rabbets should be $\frac{1}{8}$ inch wide and $\frac{1}{16}$ inch deep unless otherwise indicated.

1

2

3

4

1. Cut out the back from ⅙ inch plywood. Cut out the top lateral, two middle uprights, and two ends from your chosen wood. Cut the grooves and rabbets in the back and top lateral as indicated on Figs. 2 and 3.

2. Cut rabbets and grooves in the middle uprights and ends (see Fig. 5). Middle upright grooves should be ³⁄₁₆ inch wide. Cut six drawer runners of a thickness to match the grooves (Fig. 4).

3. Holding the top lateral and back together, insert the middle uprights into the grooves and glue in place. Use a toothpick to put glue in the drawer runner grooves on the middle uprights and insert four drawer runners. Make sure the ends of the drawer runners butt against the back and leave a gap of ³⁄₁₆ inch at the front for the front strip.

4. Insert the ends into the grooves and glue in place. Glue the two remaining drawer runners into the ends, again making sure the runners butt against the back and that there is a ³⁄₁₆ inch gap at the front.

5

5. Cut a groove ³⁄₁₆ inch deep and ⅛ inch wide right across the front of the carcass; this must exactly match the position of the grooves for the drawer runners.

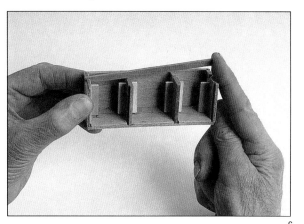

6

6. Cut the front strip (Fig. 13) and glue it into the groove in the front of the carcass. Belt or hand sand the ends and bottom of the carcass with medium sandpaper on a flat surface. The ends must be flush for gluing to the end panels and protrusions at the bottom will look untidy.

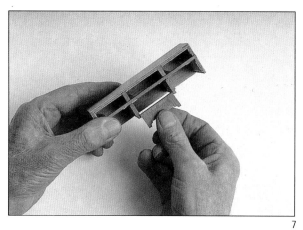

7

7. Make the apron from three pieces of wood as illustrated in Fig. 6, taking careful note of the direction of the grain on each piece. The final thickness of the apron needs to be ⅛ inch. Fit and glue the apron to the carcass.

8. Cut two side drawer bases (Fig. 7) and glue them in place in the carcass. Sand, stain and French polish the front of the carcass (see page 9).

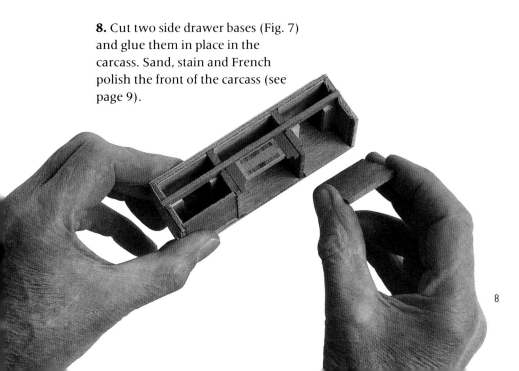

8

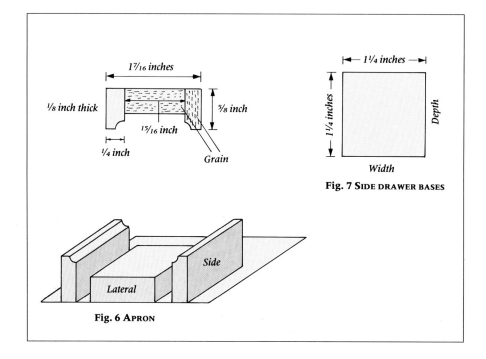

1⁷⁄₁₆ inches

⅛ inch thick

⁵⁄₈ inch

¹⁵⁄₁₆ inch

¼ inch

Grain

1¼ inches

1¼ inches

Depth

Width

Fig. 7 SIDE DRAWER BASES

Side

Lateral

Fig. 6 APRON

MAKING THE LEGS
~

9. The completed carcass.

10. Cut four legs and taper them to the measurements shown in Fig. 11 using medium sandpaper. Fine sand, stain and polish the legs. Cut two end panels to a bare ⅛ inch thick (Fig. 11). Sand, stain, and polish one side. Fit the legs to the panels and assemble on a jig. The polish should be scraped off the areas to be glued. Make sure the leg tops and the top edge of the panel are exactly aligned.

11. Cut the carcass top (Fig. 12) and glue it to the carcass. Position, but do not glue, the assembled end panels and check that the overhang of the top is equal. Check that the back of the table top aligns with the back of the carcass. Remove the end panels. Sand, stain, and polish the top. Glue the end panels in position. The back legs should be in line with the back and the front legs should protrude slightly.

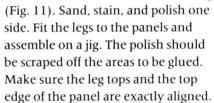

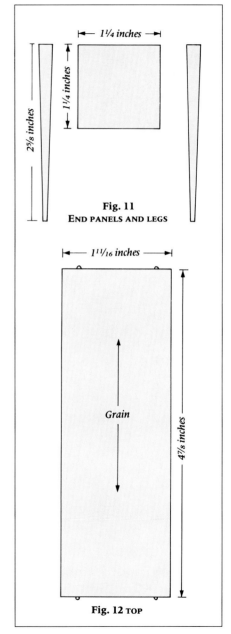

↤ 1¼ inches ↦

1¼ inches

2⅝ inches

Fig. 11
END PANELS AND LEGS

↤ 1¹¹⁄₁₆ inches ↦

Grain

4⅞ inches

Fig. 12 TOP

MAKING A SET OF DRAWERS

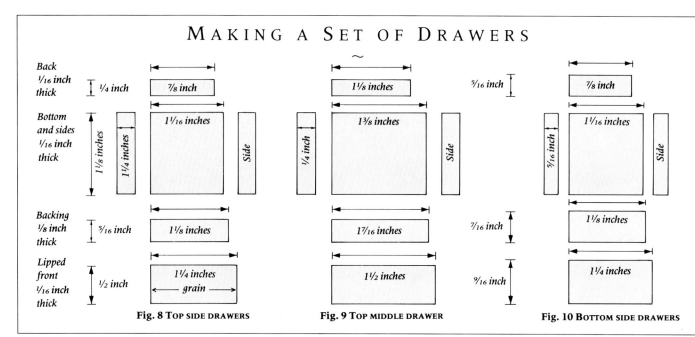

Back
1/16 inch thick

Bottom and sides 1/16 inch thick

Backing 1/8 inch thick

Lipped front 1/16 inch thick

1/4 inch

1/8 inches

1 1/4 inches

5/16 inch

1/2 inch

7/8 inch

1 1/16 inches

Side

1 1/8 inches

1 1/4 inches
grain

Fig. 8 TOP SIDE DRAWERS

~

1 1/8 inches

1 3/8 inches

Side

1 7/16 inches

1 1/2 inches

1/4 inch

Fig. 9 TOP MIDDLE DRAWER

5/16 inch

7/16 inch

9/16 inch

7/8 inch

1 1/16 inches

Side

1 1/8 inches

1 1/4 inches

5/16 inch

Fig. 10 BOTTOM SIDE DRAWERS

Cut out the drawer components – two top side drawers, two bottom side drawers, and one top middle drawer. Assemble the drawers by placing the drawer front backing piece against the back of an assembly jig. Apply glue to the front of the drawer bottom and to the backing piece. Allow the glue to set. Assemble the left side in the same way. Fit the back. Fit the drawers to the carcass. Attach the banded front. Sand the drawer fronts with medium and fine sandpaper, dust, stain and polish. Drill holes for the knobs, insert some glue and insert the knobs. Leave to dry overnight.

Shell Mirror

This mirror is a replica of a Victorian novelty.

You Will Need
~

- Cardboard or thin wood (aero-ply), 2½ × 1⅛ inches
- Marbled paper to cover
- White glue
- Thin mirror or foil, 1 × 1 inch
- 16 mouse-ear shells
- 9–10 assorted tiny, pretty shells of various shapes
- Gold felt-tipped pen for outlining handle (optional)
- 1½ inches of ⅛ inch wide narrow
- ribbon for·hanging loop

1. Cut out the shape in wood or cardboard. Pierce a hole in the handle.

2. Place the shape on marbled paper. Draw around it, leaving a margin of about ⅛ inch for the backing. Draw a second pattern to the exact shape to make the front cover.

3. Glue the cardboard or wood shape firmly to the backing paper. Smooth it with a dry, clean cloth and glue the overlap allowance down firmly on the front surface,

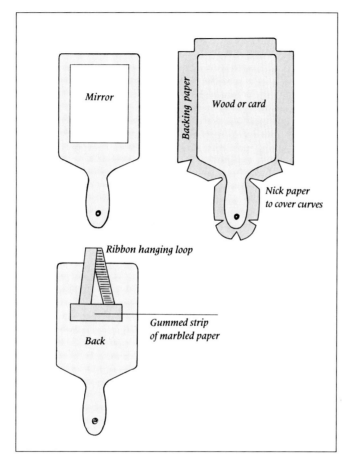

notching it with scissors on the curves.

4. Glue the front paper piece firmly in position, smoothing it with a clean, dry cloth. Glue the mirror in position on the front.

5. Draw a rough pattern of the template on plain paper and arrange the shells on it until you are happy with the design; then transfer the shells one by one to the mirror rim itself.

6. Run glue along the top edge of the mirror backing and, starting at the center, press the shells into position. Continue down the sides and along the bottom edge.

7. Outline the handle in gold.

8. Pierce through the hole in the handle. Make a small hanging loop of ribbon on the back and attach it with a piece of marbled paper if you want to hang it up.

Dollhouse

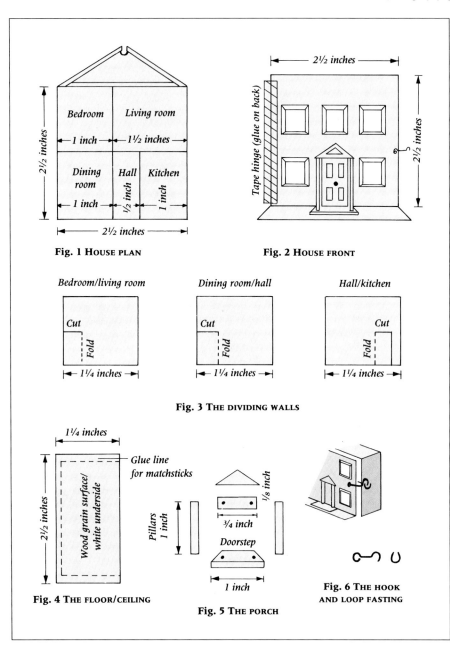

Fig. 1 HOUSE PLAN

Bedroom — 1 inch
Living room — 1½ inches
2½ inches
Dining room — 1 inch
Hall — ½ inch
Kitchen — 1 inch
2½ inches

Fig. 2 HOUSE FRONT

2½ inches
2½ inches
Tape hinge (glue on back)

Bedroom/living room
Cut
Fold
1¼ inches

Dining room/hall
Cut
Fold
1¼ inches

Hall/kitchen
Cut
Fold
1¼ inches

Fig. 3 THE DIVIDING WALLS

1¼ inches
Glue line for matchsticks
2½ inches
Wood grain surface/white underside

Fig. 4 THE FLOOR/CEILING

Pillars 1 inch
¾ inch
⅛ inch
Doorstep
1 inch

Fig. 5 THE PORCH

Fig. 6 THE HOOK AND LOOP FASTING

You Will Need

~

- Box 2½ × 2½ × 1¼ inches
- Cardboard for base 2½ × 1¾ inches
- Cardboard for pediment and porch roof, 2½ × ¾ inches
- Poster paint (ocher or gray) for pediment and body of house
- Matchsticks for pediment molding and windows
- Wood glue
- Cardboard for front, 2½ × 2½ inches
- Mat knife
- Cellophane or clear plastic for windows
- Toothpicks for pillars
- ¼ inch tape for hinges
- 1 brass bead for door knob
- Wood 1½ × ¼ inches for step

- Poster paint (black) for base and apron
- Paint (white) for door, moldings and pillars
- 3 vertical wall dividers 1¼ × 1¼ inches
- 1 horizontal floor divider 2½ × 1¼ inches
- Felt-tipped pens for decoration and detail
- Tiny scraps of wallpaper for walls and floor
- Narrow lace for curtains
- Sequins for ceiling ornaments (optional)
- Paste
- Tweezers
- Wire to make door hook
- Pliers or wire cutters

1. Find or make a suitably sized box. Cut a piece of cardboard 2¼ × 1¾ inches for the base; this is slightly larger than the house itself to form an apron at the front.

2. Trace the pediment from Fig. 1 and paint it ocher or gray. Punch out a circle from the apex and glue white-painted matchsticks in place. Glue the pediment to the top of the box.

3. Trace the front (see Fig. 2), marking the openings for the door and windows – ignore the pediment, steps, porch and pillars for the time being – and transfer them to the cardboard front. Use a sharp mat knife to cut out the windows and the door, retaining the door piece to re-attach with tape. Paint the front ocher or gray. On the other side, glue clear plastic over the windows and glue strips of lace down the sides of the windows to represent curtains. Draw on a dado, baseboard and cornice molding with felt-tipped pen and add an architrave and, if you wish, an ornament over the door.

4. On the piece cut out of the door opening glue small pieces of cardboard to represent panels on the front and attach the brass bead as the door knob. Turn over the door and stick tape along the hinge side, leaving half the width of the tape free to stick to the inside surface of the house front. Paint the back of the door any color you wish and draw on internal panels. Stick the door "hinge" in place. On the front, draw sash bars across the windows with felt-tipped pen and outline the windows. Cut matchstick moldings for the top of each window and glue in place.

5. Cut and glue the doorstep, the porch roof, the pillars and the pediment. Use felt-tipped pen to add details to these. The house illustrated has white and gold detailing, but you may prefer to use a different color.

6. Cut the room and floor dividers as in Figs. 3 and 4. Cut away the door edges and fold them back, so that the folds form hinges. Wallpaper and decorate the surfaces as you wish, then glue them in place in the house. You will probably need tweezers to hold the cardboard in place. If you glue matches close to the edges on the underside of the floor/ceiling piece, it will stick to the walls better. When the interior is finished, glue the front to the box by means of a tape hinge. Disguise the hinge by gluing a paper cover over the box before painting the outside. Varnish the exterior of the house, adding a drop of wood stain to the varnish to give it an "antique" look.

7. Make a tiny wire hook and loop with fine-gauge wire and tweezers. Pin the hook into the house front with a short dressmaker's pin, snipping off the excess shank on the inside with pliers or wire cutters. Make two small holes on the side of the house to accommodate the loop and glue the wire loop in the holes. You will have to bend the hook slightly so that it curves around the corner.

Cradle

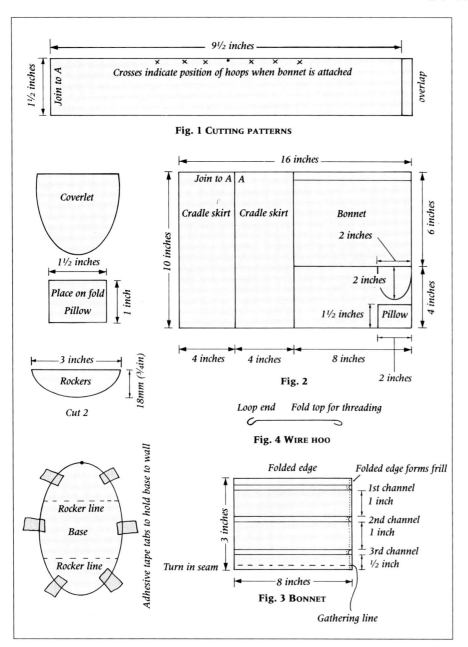

9½ inches

1½ inches

Join to A

Crosses indicate position of hoops when bonnet is attached

× × × • × × ×

overlap

Fig. 1 CUTTING PATTERNS

Coverlet

1½ inches

Place on fold
Pillow

1 inch

16 inches

Join to A | A

10 inches

Cradle skirt | *Cradle skirt* | *Bonnet*

6 inches

2 inches

2 inches

4 inches

1½ inches | *Pillow*

4 inches | **4 inches** | **8 inches**

2 inches

Fig. 2

3 inches

Rockers

18mm (¾in)

Cut 2

Loop end | *Fold top for threading*

Fig. 4 WIRE HOO

Rocker line

Base

Rocker line

Adhesive tape tabs to hold base to wall

Folded edge | *Folded edge forms frill*

1st channel
1 inch

2nd channel
1 inch

3 inches

3rd channel
½ inch

Turn in seam

8 inches

Fig. 3 BONNET

Gathering line

You Will Need

~

- Cardboard, approximately 10 × 5 inches
- Lining silk, approximately 10 × 5 inches
- ¼ inch batting, approximately 10 × 5 inches
- White cotton, approximately 14 × 10 inches
- Fabric glue
- Dressmaker's pins
- Ribbon to trim 18 inches

- Milliner's wire or strong, fine wire 15 inches
- Needlenose pliers
- Organdy, approximately 16 × 10 inches
- Lace or braid to trim, 1 yard
- ¼ inch balsawood, 3 × ¾ inches
- White enamel paint (optional)
- Sealer (to seal balsa, optional)

1. Cut a template for the cradle base and wall, and use it as a pattern to cut out the silk lining, the batting and the cotton outer covering, adding a ⅛ inch seam allowance all around for the silk and cotton pieces.

2. Cut out the pieces in cardboard and staple the foot of the cradle at the overlap. Align the dots on both pieces and glue the base to the body. You will find it easier if you position small pieces of tape under the base and use these to hold the side in place.

3. Glue a white cotton fabric cover to the outside surface of the cradle, which will make it easier to sew the lining and bonnet to the cradle. Glue the batting lightly in position inside the cradle.

4. Join the short ends of the silk cradle lining piece, then stitch it to the base. With the raw edges to the inside, drop it into position in the cradle. Fold the excess over the cradle rim and pin, then glue or sew in place.

5. Cut the bonnet pattern from the organdy. Fold the piece in half so that it measures approximately 8 × 3 inches. Sew the bottom edges – the 8 inch edge – together; the dimensions given include a ⅛ inch seam allowance. Turn to the right side and press flat. Turn under the raw edges at the open sides and catch down with small running stitches. Sew by hand or machine the three channels marked across the bonnet pieces (Fig. 3). Fasten off the ends. Use double thread to run a gathering line along the base of the piece, leaving the end sufficiently long to pull in later.

6. Cut three wire hoops, measuring 6, 5 and 4 inches. Thread the longest through the first channel, bending the bottom of the wire to form a loop that will prevent the wire from slipping into the channel, and fold the top end tightly over to stop the point of the wire from piercing or catching in the fabric. Use needlenose pliers to bend the wire. Thread the other two wires into the channels and adjust the gathers evenly. Gently arch the wires to form the bonnet shape. The finished length of the hoops should be 4½, 3½ and 2½ inches. Snip off any excess and bend back the loops. Pull the gathering line at the back of the bonnet as tight as possible and sew it to the entry point to close up the back of the bonnet. Pin the bonnet

in place on the body of the cradle, using a pin through each loop to hold it in place, then firmly sew it to the cradle.

7. Cut out the skirt strips and join them to measure 20 × 4 inches. Fold the fabric in half lengthwise. Run two rows of gathering stitches along the top open edges, pull up the gathers and pin in place, matching the center with the dot on the cradle. Arrange and pin the gathers evenly around the cradle to meet at the center back. Tie the thread. Sew or glue in place. Trim to taste. The cradle illustrated here has two rows of an organdy edging around the cradle edge to cover the raw edges of the skirt gathers and bands of organdy edging sewn over the bonnet. A pink bow has been sewn on each side of the bonnet.

8. Cut out the coverlet pieces in organdy, lining silk and batting, adding a ⅛ inch seam allowance all around for the organdy and lining silk. Baste the batting to the lining silk. Place the organdy on the lining side and sew around the edge, leaving the top open. Fasten off the thread and turn right side out. Fold in the raw edges along the top and overcast neatly. Remove all basting stitches. Trim with lace or edging.

9. Fold the pillow silk in half. Sew around the edges, leaving one side open. Turn right side out, insert the batting, sew the end edges together. Trim with lace or edging. Decorate the coverlet and pillow with bows if wished.

10. As an added extra, cut the rockers from balsawood, seal and paint with white flat-finish enamel paint. Glue them to the cradle where indicated.

Screens

You Will Need

~

- Approximately 5 × 8 inches mount card or similar
- Mat knife
- 18 inches cotton tape, ¼ inch wide, or bias binding to match screen covering
- Strong paste
- Fine sandpaper
- Satin varnish to finish

For Scrap Screen
- Lining or construction paper
- Scraps of gift wrap paper, suitable cutout pictures, etc.

For Gentleman's Screen
- Textured paper, mock leather or book binding fabric
- ¼ inch tape
- Small sets of hunting prints or suitable pictures from magazines or giftwrap

Making the Scrap Screen

1. Cut 3 panels out of cardboard.

2. Tape along one edge of two of the screen sections. The tape will act as a hinge.

3. Cut 3 panels in lining paper or construction paper. Assemble the cutout scraps and arrange them on each panel. When you have decided on the design, glue them to the panels, overlapping them to cover the backing paper completely.

4. Glue the decorated panels to the cardboard panels. Press firmly and smooth with a dry, clean cloth. When the glue is dry, check that all the glued areas are stuck down.

5. Varnish the panels. Leave to dry for a few hours. Sand lightly with fine sandpaper and apply a second coat of varnish. Repeat the sanding process and apply a third coat. If you wish, mix a drop of wood stain with the final coat of varnish to give an antique finish.

Making the Gentleman's Screen

1. Cut 4 panels out of strong cardboard. Cut 2 panels in textured paper, adding ⅛ inch on three sides and two panels allowing ⅛ inch at the top and bottom. Cut 4 panels for the front of the screen.

2. Glue 4½ inches of tape down the outside edge of 3 of the 4 cardboard panels to act as hinges.

3. Spread glue evenly over the paper panels and the extra allowances. Cover the cardboard panels with paper.

4. The panels with the allowance at the top and bottom will be in the center of the finished screen. Those with allowances on three edges will be at each end.

5. Join the screen by taping the adjoining panels together. Glue the 4 front panels of paper to the front of the screen and decorate each panel with suitable prints, placing 3 or 4 on each panel. When they are firmly glued, varnish as for the scrap screen.

If the panels curl after decorating, place between two boards and clamp, leaving overnight, to flatten.

4½ inches at curve

Cut 3 in card

Cut 3 in lining paper

3¾ inches

Glue tape for hinge

Adjoining panel

2 inches

Fig. 1 SCRAP SCREEN

4¾ inches

Cut 4 in card

Cut 4 in paper

Cut 2 with 3 side allowance, cut 2 with top and bottom allowance

Backing paper   4½ inches

Tape hinge

Adjoining panel

2 inches

Fig. 2 GENTLEMAN'S SCREEN

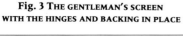

Backing paper

Card

Tape

Fig. 3 THE GENTLEMAN'S SCREEN WITH THE HINGES AND BACKING IN PLACE

THE DINING ROOM

~

Regency Dining Table

~

A beautiful reproduction table which will be the focus of any dining room. The construction of the legs – molded column, leg holder and separate legs – is complex, but is much more elegant than the standard four-leg construction. You can of course simplify the molding on the leg columns and leg holder.

~

MAKING THE TABLE TOP

~

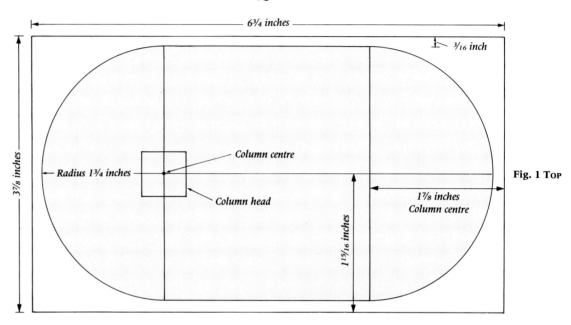

Fig. 1 Top

1

1. Cut a rectangular blank ⅛ inch thick to the measurements shown in Fig. 1. Mark the shape of the table top and the horizontal and vertical lines; use a pencil so that you can erase the lines when you have completed the table.

2

2. Cut one of the straight edges, then a "D-end," then the second side, and finally the other D-end.

MAKING THE LEG COLUMNS

~

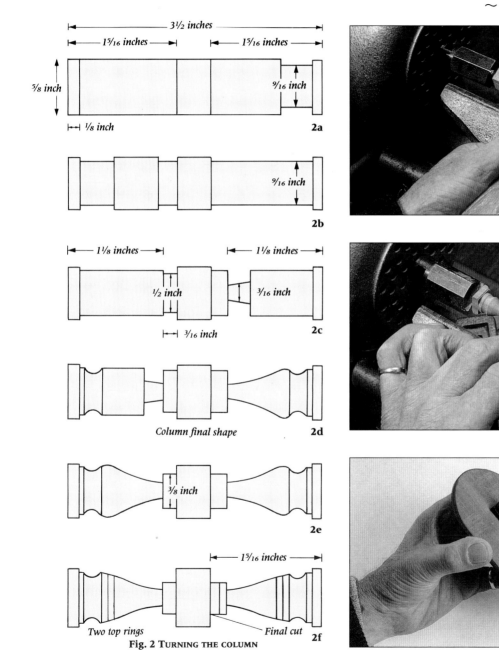

5/8 inch

3½ inches

1⁵/₁₆ inches — 1⁵/₁₆ inches

⁹/₁₆ inch

⅛ inch

2a

⁹/₁₆ inch

2b

1⅛ inches — 1⅛ inches

½ inch — ³/₁₆ inch

³/₁₆ inch

2c

Column final shape **2d**

³/₈ inch

2e

1⁵/₁₆ inches

Two top rings — *Final cut* **2f**

Fig. 2 TURNING THE COLUMN

3. Cut a square-ended blank – one blank makes two columns – to the dimensions shown in Fig. 2a. The leg columns will then need to be shaped according to the sequence shown (Figs. 2b–e).

3

4. Hand sand the columns. Cut the two top rings (Fig. 2f). Cut the ring on the pad. Dust, stain and French polish the columns. Cut the columns to their final length – 1⁵/₁₆ inches.

4

5. Assemble the columns and the table top.

5

6. Dust, sand and polish the table top.

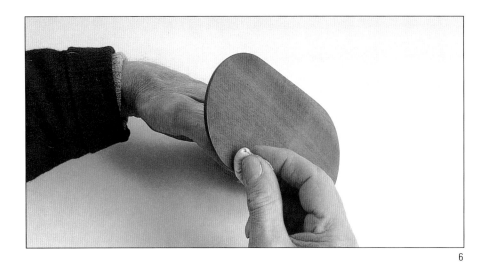

6

MAKING THE LEG HOLDERS

~

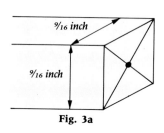

Fig. 3a

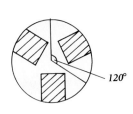

Fig. 3d CUTTING SLOTS

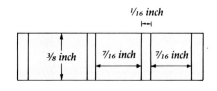

Fig. 3b BLANK TURNED TO ⅜IN DIAMETER

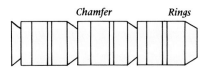

Fig. 3c RUNNING CHAMFER AND RINGS

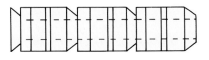

Fig. 3d CUTTING SLOTS

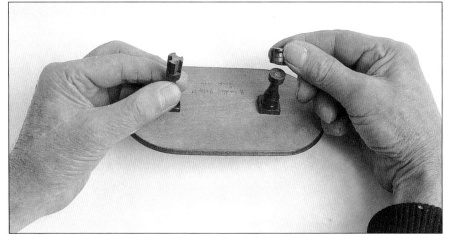

7

7. Cut a square-ended blank (Fig. 3a) and turn it so that it is ⅜ inch in diameter (Fig. 3b). Cut rings and a chamfer (Fig. 3c). Stain and polish the pieces. Cut three slots down the sides of the piece at 120° to each other (Fig. 3d). Make the final cuts to give a length of ⁷⁄₁₆ inch. Assemble the leg holders to the columns.

MAKING THE LEGS

~

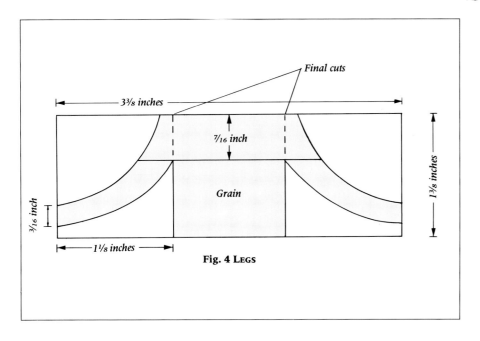

3⅜ inches

Final cuts

⁷⁄₁₆ inch

1⅜ inches

³⁄₁₆ inch

Grain

1⅛ inches

Fig. 4 LEGS

8. You will need six legs for one table – a pair of legs is cut from one slice. You may want to use the pinned blank method (see page 10), illustrated here, to guarantee uniformity of the pieces you cut. Test the width of leg required against the slots cut in step 7, and cut the slices (Fig. 4) to this width.

9. Draw the leg shape on a slice, or just the top slice if using a pinned blank, and cut out the number of pieces required.

8

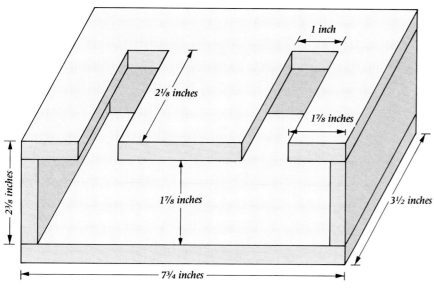

1 inch

2⅛ inches

1⅞ inches

2⅜ inches

1⅞ inches

3½ inches

7¾ inches

Fig. 5 FINAL ASSEMBLY JIG

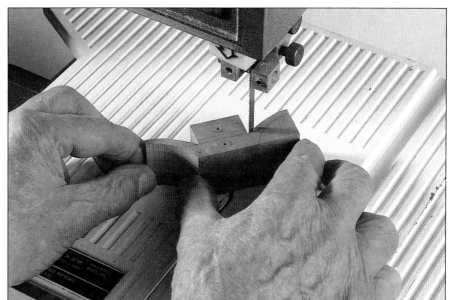

9

10. Sand the top surfaces of the pieces, or pinned blank. Keep checking the finished height of the legs against the assembly jig (Fig. 5). Do not forget to tidy the underside of the legs. Using medium and fine sandpaper and working by hand, shape and surface. Stain and polish these surfaces.

11. Dismantle the pinned blank, if used, and check the height of the legs in the jig. Taper the legs with medium and fine sandpaper, stain and polish. Make the final cuts (Fig. 4) to the legs and fit the legs to the leg holders.

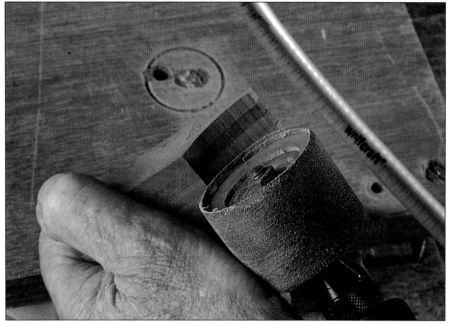

10

12. When you are satisfied with the height of the table, by checking against the jig, glue the legs in position in the leg holders and leave to dry overnight.

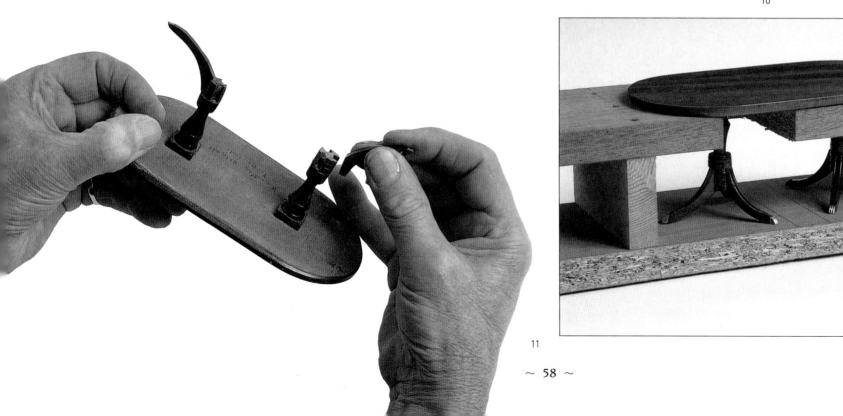

11

12

Chairs

~

Two delightful variations on the same design – a side chair and a carving chair for the head of the table – which complement the dining table design perfectly. To make sure that all four legs of your finished chairs touch the floor, choose sides that match as exactly as possible and use the special assembly jig described.

~

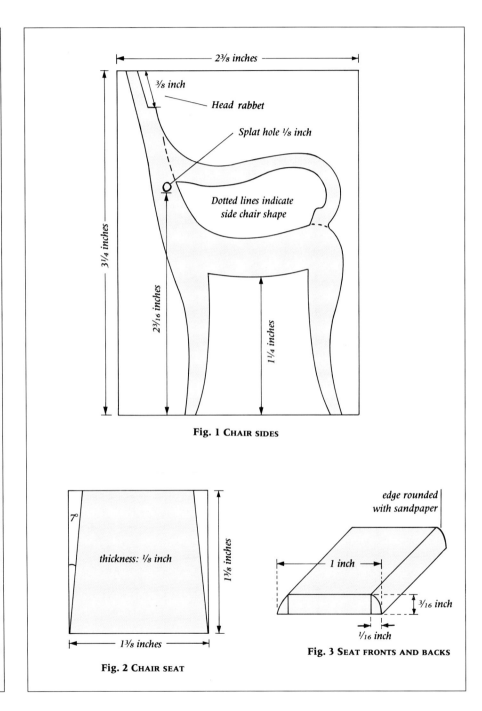

2⅜ inches

⅜ inch

Head rabbet

Splat hole ⅛ inch

Dotted lines indicate side chair shape

3¼ inches

2³⁄₁₆ inches

1¼ inches

Fig. 1 CHAIR SIDES

7°

thickness: ⅛ inch

1⅜ inches

1⅜ inches

Fig. 2 CHAIR SEAT

edge rounded with sandpaper

1 inch

³⁄₁₆ inch

¹⁄₁₆ inch

Fig. 3 SEAT FRONTS AND BACKS

1

1. Cut slices for the chair sides to the measurements shown in Fig. 1. Make the slices ⅛ inch wide. Belt or hand sand both sides of the slices. Draw the chair shapes on the slices. If you are making several chairs at once, use the pinned blank method (see page 10). Cut out the sides.

2

2. For the carving chair, you need to drill a hole in the center of the arm as a point of entry for the saw. Finish cutting out the chair.

3

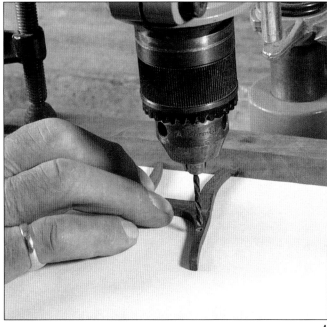

4

3. Sand all the surfaces. Keep the sides in matching pairs – mark this on the inside surface. Stain and polish all the surfaces which will show, including the underside of the arms. Slightly round the front edges of the sides with sandpaper.

4. Drill ⅛ inch holes for the splats (decorative lateral pieces) as shown in Fig. 1.

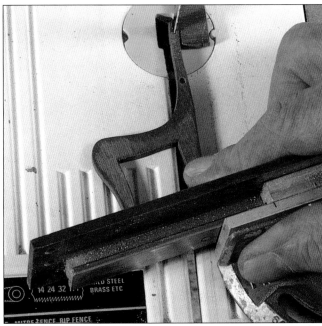

5

6

5. Cut a rabbet in the top of each side to hold the head (Fig. 1).

6. Cut the seat in pine (Fig. 2). Make the seat backs and fronts – cut a section ³⁄₁₆ inch wide and 1 inch deep and the length of the seat. Hand sand both edges to give a rounded effect (Fig. 3). Stain and polish. Cut the fronts to 1¾ inches and the backs to 1¼ inches. Glue to the seat and trim the ends. When the glue is dry, sand the edges of the seat so that the edgings are flush.

MAKING THE ASSEMBLY JIG

~

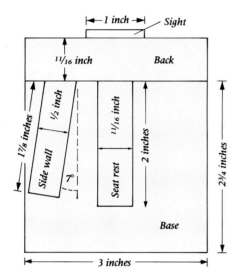

Fig. 4 ASSEMBLY JIG PLAN

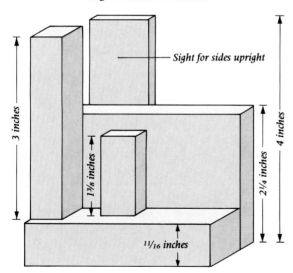

Fig. 4a ASSEMBLY JIG FRONT ELEVATION

Cut the base and mark the positions of the side wall and seat rest. Cut the back, and pin and glue it to the base. Check that it is vertical with a small carpenter's square. Cut the side wall and seat rest pieces. Glue the side wall to the base and back. Check the vertical with a carpenter's square. Cut the "sight" piece and pin and glue it to the back. Check the vertical.

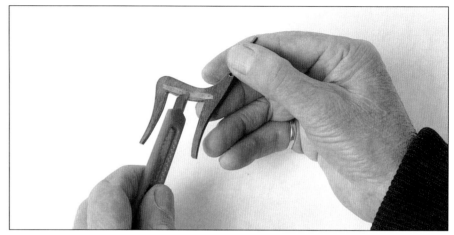

7

7. Scrape the inside area of the sides where they will be glued to the seat edges.

8. Place the left side of the chair flat against the side wall of the jig. Put glue on the left side of the seat. Place the seat on the seat rest and glue to the sides so that the front edge of the seat is $1/16$ inch in from the front of the side. When the glue has set, place the right side on the jig, lining it up with the jig sighter, but do not glue.

8

MAKING THE SPLAT

~

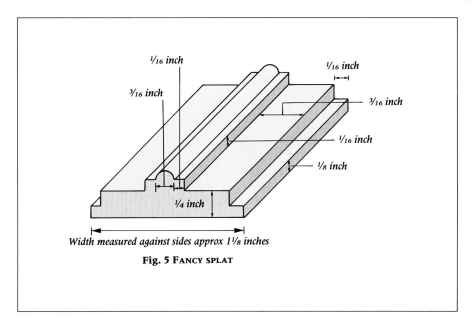

Fig. 5 **FANCY SPLAT**

Width measured against sides approx 1⅛ inches

¹/₁₆ inch

³/₁₆ inch

¹/₁₆ inch

³/₁₆ inch

¹/₁₆ inch

⅛ inch

¼ inch

10

10. In this case, a whole section has been molded to the shape of the splat, so thin sections have to be sliced off to a width of slightly more than ¹/₁₆ inch. Hand sand, stain and polish the back of the strips. Drill a ¹/₁₆ inch hole in the center of the splat for decoration.

9

9. Next, make the splat (Fig. 5). This can be straight or a more ornamented one as illustrated.

11

11. You may need to trim the ends of the splats to get a snug fit in the sides. Insert glue in the holes and assemble the splat to the left-hand side on the jig. Place the right side on the jig and insert the other end of the splat in the hole. Check that all the legs are flat on the jig base.

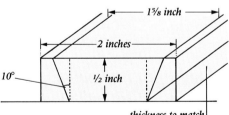

12. Cut the head to thickness of the rabbet cut in the chair side (Fig. 6). Glue the head in position, making sure that the overhang is even at both ends.

1⅝ inch

2 inches

½ inch

10°

Fig. 6 Chair head

thickness to match rebate cut in sides

Making the Upholstered Seat
~

cut one in ⅛ inch padding
cut one in ⅙ inch plywood

1¼ inches

7°

1¼ inches

Fig. 7 Plywood base

1½ inches

2⅝ inches

1⅞ inches

2⅝ inches

2¼ inches

Fig. 8 Seat material

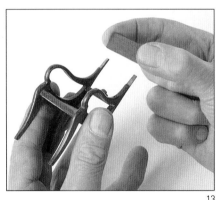

13. Cut a seat shape from ⅙ inch plywood to the measurements in Fig. 7. Cut out a piece of foam or padding the same size. Glue the padding to the plywood. Cut out fabric using the pattern in Fig. 8. Cover the seat with the fabric and glue the edges in place. Glue onto the chair.

Sideboard

~

This design, although similar to the dresser and desk in basic construction, has a slightly longer top and two central legs to give stability. The large surface area of the sides and top must be finished very carefully, using at least eight coats of polish for a truly professional result.

~

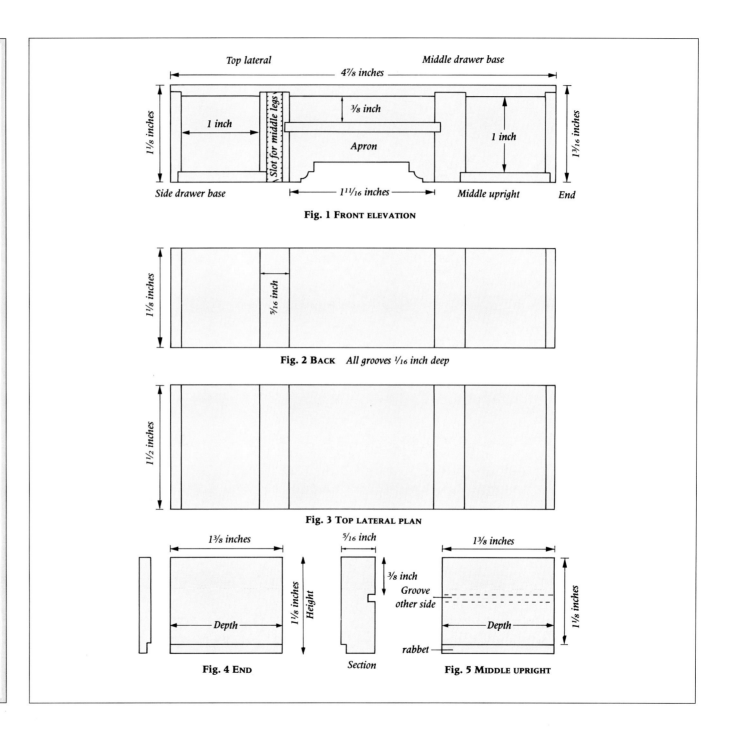

Fig. 1 FRONT ELEVATION

Fig. 2 BACK   All grooves 1/16 inch deep

Fig. 3 TOP LATERAL PLAN

Fig. 4 END   Section   Fig. 5 MIDDLE UPRIGHT

1. Cut the back from ⅙ inch plywood. Cut the top lateral, from your chosen wood, to ⅛ inch thick. Make grooves and rabbets as shown in Figs. 2 and 3. All grooves should be 1/16 inch deep.

2. Cut two middle uprights to the dimensions shown in Fig. 5. Make a 1/16 inch groove to one side and a ⅛ inch rabbet on the other side. Cut two ends ⅛ inch thick as shown in Fig. 4. Make a rabbet in the ends.

3. Make slots 3/16 inch wide and ⅛ inch deep in the middle uprights for the middle legs.

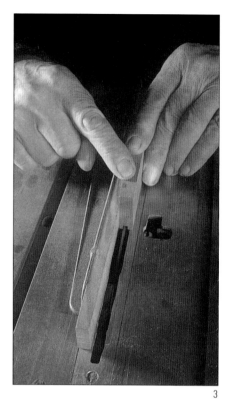

1
2
3

4. Assemble the back, top lateral and middle uprights of the carcass on a jig. Apply glue to the grooves on the back, the middle upright and the top edge. Glue the top of the lateral to the top edge of the back. Glue the middle uprights to the back and top lateral. Allow the glue to dry.

5. Apply glue to the rabbets for the ends on the back and top lateral and glue the ends in place. Allow the glue to dry.

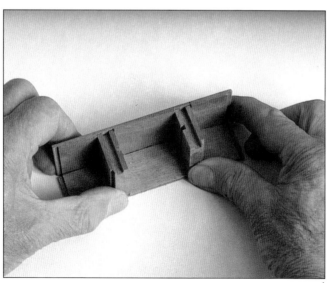
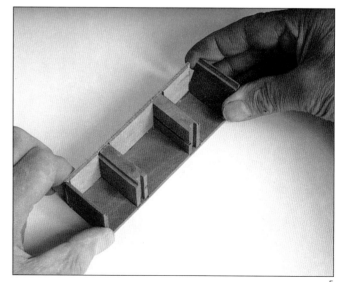

4
5

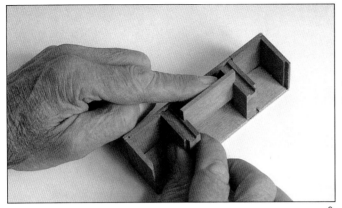

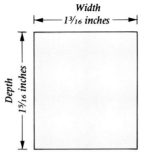

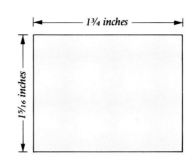

Width
1³/₁₆ inches

Depth
1⁵/₁₆ inches

1³/₄ inches

1⁵/₁₆ inches

Fig. 6 SIDE DRAWER – BASE **Fig. 7 MIDDLE DRAWER – BASE**

6. Cut out one base ⅛ inch thick for the middle drawer and two bases ⅛ inch thick for the side drawers (Figs. 6 and 7). Sand the ends and bottom of the carcass on medium paper on a flat surface. The ends must be flush for gluing the end panels.

1¹¹/₁₆ inches

¼ inch

1³/₁₆ inches

⅝ inch

Fig. 8 APRON

7. Next cut the apron. You will need a rectangular block of wood for the central piece 1³/₁₆ × ⅜ inches and at least 1½ inches long. Cut two pieces ⅝ × ¼ inch for the side pieces to the same length; these will have to be shaped as shown (Fig. 8).

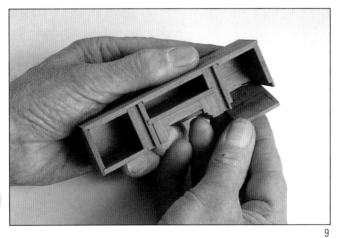

8. Glue the apron components together and slice off a piece ⅛ inch thick .

9. Fit and glue the apron and drawer bases to the carcass. Sand the front of the carcass on a sheet of medium sandpaper on a flat surface so that all the front members are flush, dust off, stain and French polish.

MAKING THE LEGS
~

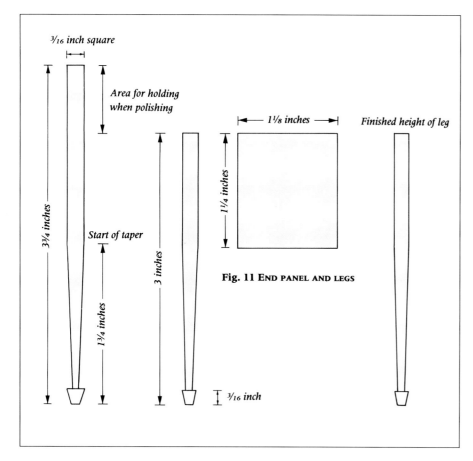

¾/16 inch square

Area for holding
when polishing

Start of taper

3¾ inches

1¾ inches

3 inches

1⅛ inches

1¼ inches

Finished height of leg

¾/16 inch

Fig. 11 END PANEL AND LEGS

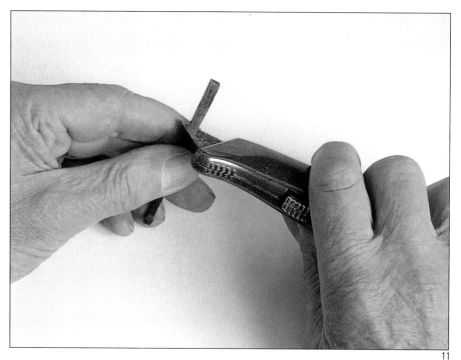

11

11. The inside of the legs and parts of the panels to be glued to the carcass should be scraped with a mat knife to remove all polish; otherwise, the glue will not stick.

12. Glue the middle legs to the carcass. Make sure all the legs touch the floor.

10. For the legs, you will need six square blanks. Taper the legs to the shape shown in Fig. 11. Fine sand, dust, stain and polish the legs. Cut the legs to the finished length. Cut two end panels ⅛ inch thick. Sand, dust, stain and polish one side. Assemble the legs and end panels on a jig. Make sure the leg tops and the top of the panel align exactly.

10

12

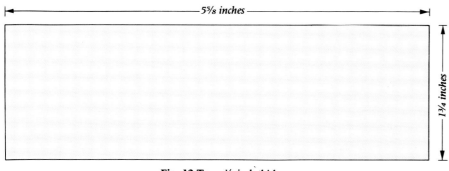

← 5⅝ inches →

1¾ inches

Fig. 12 TOP ⅛ *inch thick*

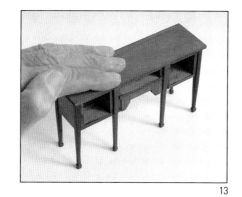

13

13. Cut out the top (Fig. 12). Apply glue to the top of the carcass and position the top. Test the end panels for fit. Remove the end panels. When the glue is completely dry, dust, stain, and polish the table top. Glue the end panels in position. The back legs line up with the back and the front legs protrude slightly.

MAKING THE DRAWERS
~

← 1⁷⁄₁₆in →

¼in

¼ inch   **Back**   ¼ inch

← 1⅝ inches →

1¼ inches   **Bottom and sides**

← 1¹¹⁄₁₆ inches →

⅜ inch   **Backing**

← 1⅞ inches →

½ inch   **Lipped front**

Fig. 9 MIDDLE DRAWER

¾ inch

¾ inch   **Back**

¾ inch   1⁵⁄₁₆ inch   ¾ inch

Bottom and sides

1⁵⁄₁₆ inch   1 inch   **Backing**

1⅛ inches   1⅛ inches   **Lipped front**

Fig. 10 SIDE DRAWERS

14

14. Cut out components for two side drawers and one middle drawer. To construct a drawer, place the drawer front backing piece against the vertical back of the jig. Apply glue to the front of the drawer bottom and the backing piece. Apply glue to the front and bottom of the right-hand side. Allow the glue to dry and assemble the left side.

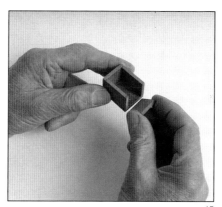

15

15. Fit the back by applying glue to both sides and bottom, and assemble. Fit the drawer to the carcass.

16. The lipped drawer front should overlap all the drawer edges by 1/16 inch. You can test this against a rabbet 1/16 inch deep run in a piece of scrap. Drill a hole in the center of the drawers for the knobs and glue the knobs in place.

16

Mantelpiece

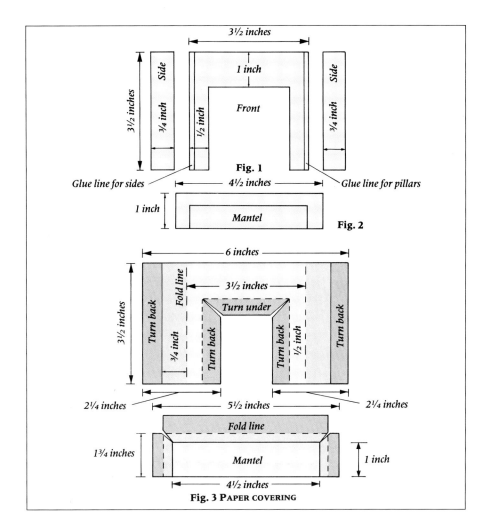

3½ inches

Side

3½ inches

¾ inch

½ inch

1 inch

Front

Side

¾ inch

Fig. 1

Glue line for sides

4½ inches

Glue line for pillars

1 inch

Mantel

Fig. 2

6 inches

Turn back

Fold line

3½ inches

Turn under

Turn back

3½ inches

¾ inch

Turn back

Turn back

½ inch

Turn back

2¼ inches

5½ inches

2¼ inches

Fold line

1¾ inches

Mantel

1 inch

4½ inches

Fig. 3 PAPER COVERING

You Will Need
~

- Wood (pine, obeche or similar) for sides 3½ × 5 × ⅛ inches; for mantel 1 × 4½ × ³⁄₁₆ inches
- ¼ inch dowel, 2 pieces each 3½ inches
- Marbled paper to cover wood
- Wood adhesive

1. Cut the wood pieces. Glue the side pieces to the back. When the glue is dry, stick marbled paper over the front and sides. Smooth the covering firmly with a clean, dry cloth.

2. Cover the mantel piece with marbled paper and glue it firmly to the sides.

3. Cover the two pieces of dowel with paper; you will need about 1 × 3½ inches of paper for each pillar. When the glue is dry, run a line of glue down each side of the surround as indicated on Fig. 1. Put a spot of glue on top of the pillars and press them into position, holding them in place until dry.

4. Your mantel piece can now be glued in place in your dollhouse or room setting. Glue a piece of contrasting marbled paper over a hearth made from a piece of cardboard measuring approximately 4½ × 2 inches to complement the finished mantel piece.

French-style Metal Chandelier

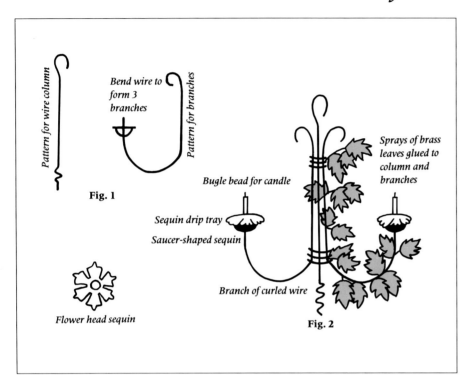

Pattern for wire column

Bend wire to form 3 branches

Pattern for branches

Fig. 1

Bugle bead for candle

Sequin drip tray

Saucer-shaped sequin

Flower head sequin

Branch of curled wire

Sprays of brass leaves glued to column and branches

Fig. 2

You Will Need
~

- Strong wire for branches, three pieces, each approximately 4 inches
- Needlenose pliers
- Strong wire for the column, 3 inches
- Fine wire for lashings
- Superglue gel
- Brass foliage (available in sheets from craft suppliers)
- Enamel gloss paint (2 shades of green)
- Tweezers
- 3 flower-shaped, mother-of-pearl sequins for candle drip trays
- 3 saucer-shaped sequins or brass jewelry findings
- 3 glass bugle beads for candles
- approximately 6 inches of ribbon ⅛ inch-wide

1. Bend the three branches into shape with needlenose pliers, using Fig. 1 as a guide. Bind these tightly to the column with fine wire, spacing them evenly around the column. Hang the skeleton from a craft stand or "third hand" and, after checking that the branches are correctly spaced, apply some glue to the lashings to hold the branches firm. Paint column and branches green.

2. Cut off a quarter of a sheet of leaves (ivy leaves were used here) and use two shades of green to paint the leaves to give the effect of light and shade. When the paint is dry, turn the sheet over and repeat on the other side.

3. When the paint is dry, cut the leaves free from the sheet and bend them into natural shapes. Glue sprays of leaves to the branches and column with superglue. Use tweezers to press them into position if necessary.

4. When the glue has set, thread the "saucer" sequins onto the branches, making sure that they do not drop too far down. Hold them in position until the glue has set. Add a flower-head sequin to each branch, followed by a bugle bead. Snip off any excess wire and dab the tip of the wire with superglue to stop the beads from falling off.

5. Fold the ribbon in half and knot the ends together. Hang the chandelier from this ribbon, suspended from a ceiling hook in the doll's house.

Four-Branch Chandelier

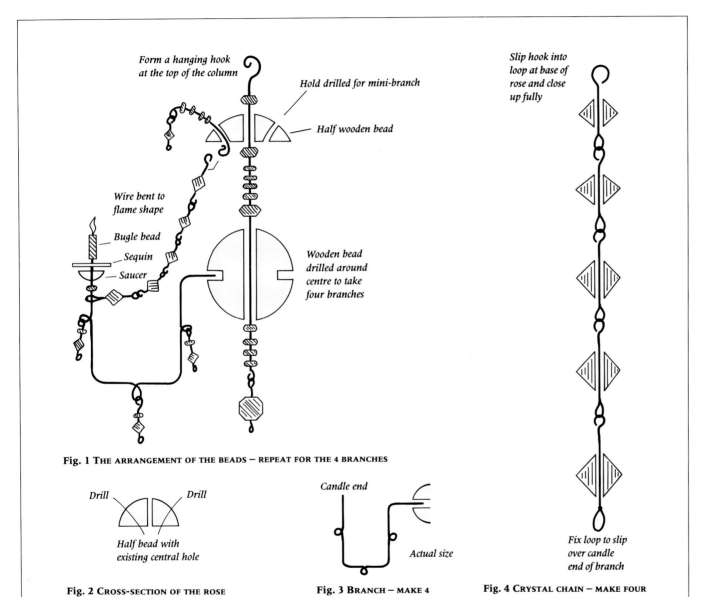

Form a hanging hook
at the top of the column

Hold drilled for mini-branch

Half wooden bead

Wire bent to
flame shape

Bugle bead

Sequin

Saucer

Wooden bead
drilled around
centre to take
four branches

Fig. 1 THE ARRANGEMENT OF THE BEADS – REPEAT FOR THE 4 BRANCHES

Drill   Drill

Half bead with
existing central hole

Fig. 2 CROSS-SECTION OF THE ROSE

Candle end

Actual size

Fig. 3 BRANCH – MAKE 4

Slip hook into
loop at base of
rose and close
up fully

Fix loop to slip
over candle
end of branch

Fig. 4 CRYSTAL CHAIN – MAKE FOUR

You Will Need
~

- 48 small clear-glass beads for the column and the 4 crystal-bearing mini-branches
- 4 fat-ended crystal cut beads for central column (the one at the bottom should be slightly larger)
- 20 facet-cut (crystal) beads for crystal chains
- 4 facet-cut (crystal) beads for mini-branches at rose level
- 12 facet-cut (crystal) beads for drops on main branches
- 4 sequins for drip trays
- 4 concave jewelry findings for base of drip trays (optional)
- Strong wire for column and branches
- Finer craft wire for chain links and to hook beads to each other
- 2 large wooden beads, ¾ inch, to make the rose and bulbous base
- Thick gold felt-tipped pen to color beads
- Spiral drill for drilling holes through the rose and ball base to take the wire branches
- Small saw for cutting the wooden beads in half
- Needlenose pliers for bending wires to shape and cutting to required length
- Tweezers to twist chain link ends together.

1. Cut one of the large wooden beads in half. Drill four holes diagonally through the domed shape at equal intervals (Fig. 2). Color this with the gold pen.

2. Pass a 1¼ inches length of wire through each hole and bend the bottom end of each wire emerging from the flat undersurface of the bead into a closed loop (Fig. 1). In Fig. 1 each bead is shown widely spaced for clarity. On the end of each branch emerging from the curved top surface, thread four small clear-glass beads. Bend the wire into a closed loop, snipping off any excess with pliers. Thread one crystal bead onto fine wire, make a small loop at one end to keep the bead on, bend the other end into a hook, snipping off the excess, then hang the crystal drop from the loop on the mini-branch. Repeat for the other three branches.

3. Cut strong wire to form a column 2½ inches long. Bend the top into a hanging hook, then thread on one flat-ended crystal, the half wooden rose bead, one flat-ended crystal bead, four plain clear-glass, and one flat-ended crystal bead.

4. Before continuing, drill four holes horizontally through the second wooden bead, spacing them evenly around the bead (Fig. 1), and color it gold. Use the existing hole to

thread this on the column and then add four clear glass beads. Form the wire into a closed loop and trim off the excess. Then thread one large crystal bead onto a short wire, forming a short loop to keep the bead on the wire. Bend the wire at the other end into a hook and hang from the loop on the column.

5. Make four wire branches using the outline in Fig. 3 as a guide for size and shape. Using superglue to glue each branch firmly into the four drilled holes in the round bead. You will find it easier to work if you hang the chandelier from a craft stand. Thread drops of one plain bead and one crystal on thin wire and hang them from the three loops formed on each of the four branches (this will take 12 such drops). Make four chains of finer wire with five crystal beads each (Fig. 4). Twist the ends of the loops well to secure. Hook one end of each chain to the loops on the underside of the rose and twist shut, slip the loops at the other end over the candle-bearing ends of the branches.

6. When all the chains are in place, thread a "saucer" (optional) and sequin over each branch, topping each with a bugle bead. Bend the excess wire to form a flame and snip off the excess. For extra length, hang the chandelier on a ribbon or chain from the ceiling hook.

Bookshelves

~

These pretty shelves have a similar side design to the hanging shelves, but the use of a mahogany-style wood gives the piece a more substantial, old-fashioned look suitable for a living room. Since the back is visible and decorative, it needs to have the same level of finish as the sides and shelves; it can be made either with solid mahogany or with a mixture of plywood-backed veneer and mahogany.

~

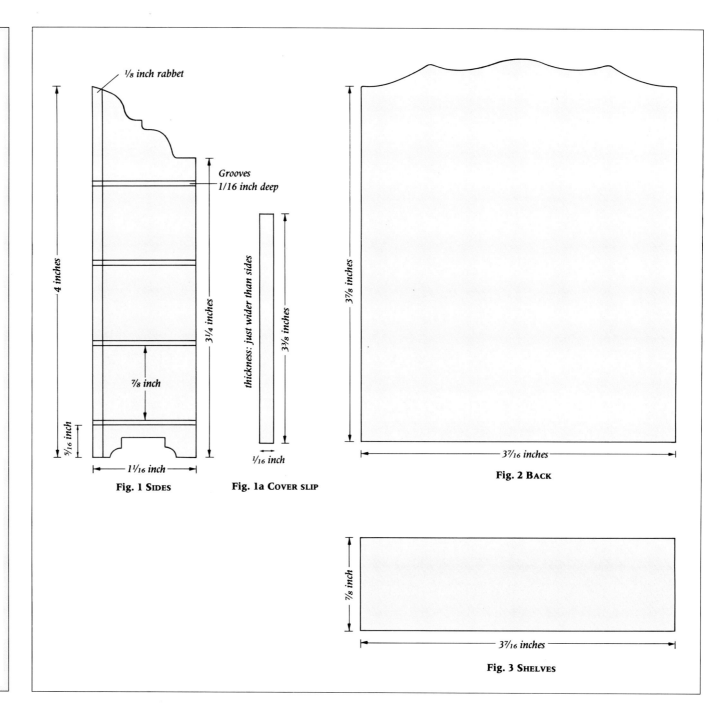

1/8 inch rabbet

Grooves 1/16 inch deep

4 inches

3 1/4 inches

7/8 inch

5/16 inch

1 1/16 inch

Fig. 1 SIDES

thickness: just wider than sides

3 3/8 inches

1/16 inch

Fig. 1a COVER SLIP

3 7/8 inches

3 7/16 inches

Fig. 2 BACK

7/8 inch

3 7/16 inches

Fig. 3 SHELVES

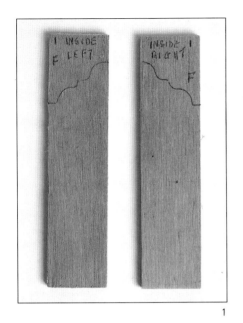

1

2

3

4

5

1. Cut slices for the sides measuring 1 × 4½ inches and ⅛ inch thick. Mark whether the side is an inside left or inside right. Draw the shape of the sides in pencil (Fig. 1).

2. Make shelf grooves and rabbets. Cut two cover slips (Fig. 1a) and glue them to the front edges of the sides. Sand the edges so the slips are flush with the outside surface of the blanks. Stain and polish the inside surface of the blank. Cut out the sides. You may wish to use the pinned blank method (page 10) if you are using power tools.

3. Two polished sides with the grooves and rabbets ready cut. Cut the shelves to a thickness to match the grooves in the sides (Fig. 3). Stain and polish one surface and the front edge of the shelves. Stain, but do not polish, the underside of the shelves.

4. Cut out a blank for the back to a thickness of ⅛ inch (Fig. 2). Mark the head shape in pencil. Stain and polish the surface.

5. Cut the head shape. Sand, stain and polish the top of the head shape. Insert glue into the grooves and both rabbets on the sides.

Alternative Methods
~

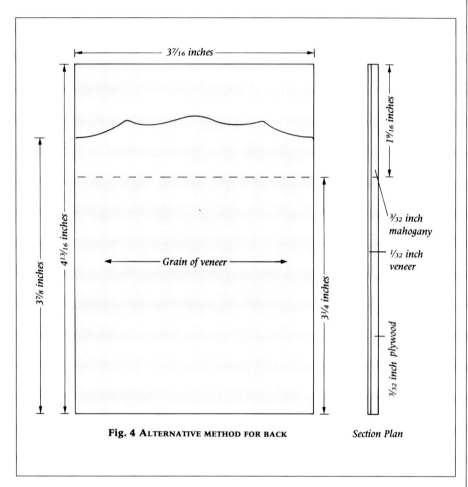

Fig. 4 ALTERNATIVE METHOD FOR BACK   *Section Plan*

If you are using power tools, you may find it difficult to cut the head shape due to the thinness of the wood. Instead, you can use a combination of plywood and your chosen wood covered with a veneer. The head shape is cut in the good-quality wood, so that the top edge can be finished properly. Glue the two sections of wood together to form one sheet and glue on the veneer, with the grain running across the width. Hand sand and dust. Mark the head shape and stain and polish the veneered surface to about ¼ inch beyond the outline of the head shape. Leave to dry. Cut the head shape.

6. Place the right side on the jig with the feet against the adjacent jig wall. Place the back on the jig to engage the back rabbet. Position the back so that the top of the side-shaped head and the top of the back head align.

7. Insert the shelves so that they are at right angles to one side. Add the left side, engaging the bottom shelf first and working upward. Leave the glue to dry. Fine sand, stain and polish the outside surfaces of the sides.

7

Desk

~

The desk is smaller and squarer than either the sideboard and the dresser, but it is very similar in design. The main difference is the use of molded strips of wood – "upstands" – to decorate the top surface; these strips are inserted into grooves on three sides of the top and give the piece a distinctive appearance.

~

All pieces 3mm (⅛in) thick unless otherwise stated

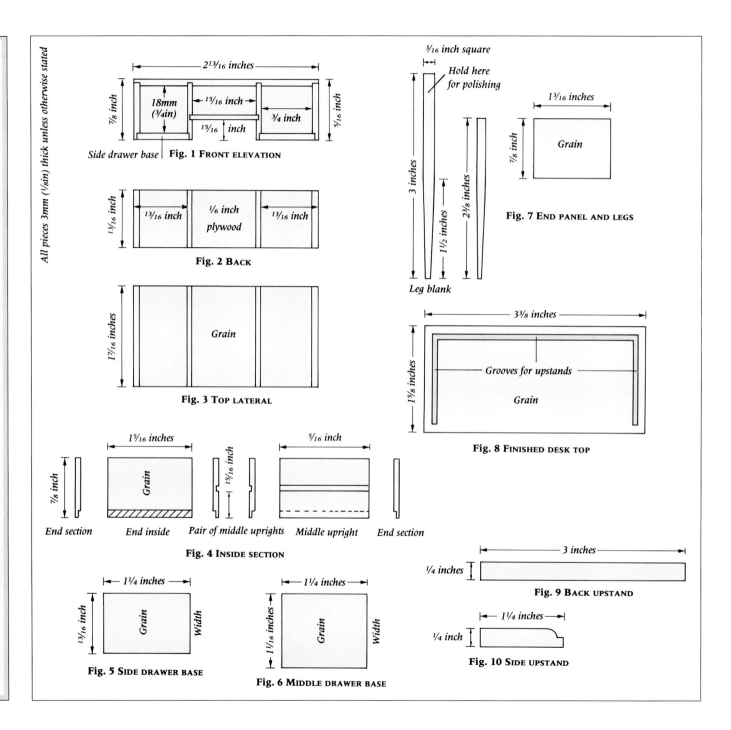

Side drawer base | **Fig. 1** FRONT ELEVATION

Fig. 2 BACK

Fig. 3 TOP LATERAL

Fig. 4 INSIDE SECTION

End section End inside Pair of middle uprights Middle upright End section

Fig. 5 SIDE DRAWER BASE

Fig. 6 MIDDLE DRAWER BASE

Fig. 7 END PANEL AND LEGS

Leg blank

Fig. 8 FINISHED DESK TOP

Grooves for upstands

Fig. 9 BACK UPSTAND

Fig. 10 SIDE UPSTAND

1. Cut out the back from ⅙ inch plywood. Cut the top lateral, the side drawer bases, the carcass ends, the middle uprights, and the end panels all to a thickness of ⅛ inch; cut the middle drawer base to a thickness of ¹⁄₁₆ inch. Run ¹⁄₁₆ inch grooves and rabbets in all these pieces as indicated. Glue the back, top lateral and middle uprights in place. Sand all the edges flush. Glue the ends in place.

2. Sand, stain, and polish the front of the carcass. Assemble the bases for all the drawers. Make four square-ended blanks for the legs. Use medium sandpaper to taper the legs, starting at the point indicated on Fig. 7. Sand, stain and polish the legs. Cut the legs to their final length.

3. Assemble the legs and end panels on a jig. Scrape away the polish from any surfaces to be glued. Make sure the leg tops and the top of the panel are exactly aligned.

4. Cut the top (Fig. 8) to ⅛ inch. Cut ¹⁄₁₆ inch grooves ³⁄₁₆ inch away from the back and side edges of the desk top for the "upstands." Position, but do not glue, the assembled end panels to the carcass. Glue the top in position.

5. Cut two strips ¼ × 3½ inches and the thickness of the grooves in the top (Fig. 9). These will form the upstands to go around the edge of the top.

6. Polish one strip for the back upstand, holding one end. Hold the second strip in the middle and polish both ends. Leave the polish to harden overnight.

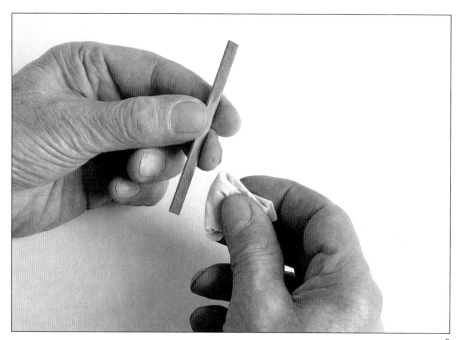

5

7. Cut the second upstand strip to form two 1¼ inches lengths. Test the strips against the side grooves and cut if necessary. Mold the front ends of the side upstand pieces (Fig. 10). Sand and stain the molding and retouch the polish.

7

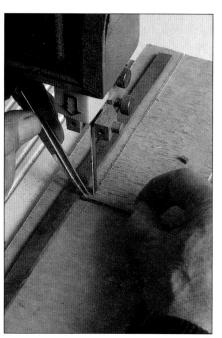

8

8. To cut two end stops for the front of the desk, cut a section 1 × 7⁄16 × 7⁄16 inches and slice it to the width of the grooves in the top. Cut a strip slightly wider than the depth of the grooves, and along the grain. Now cut four stops from the leftover strip for the other ends of the grooves; these need to be the width of the grooves and 3⁄16 inch long.

9. Dry-assemble the upstands to the desk top. Insert glue in the grooves for the stops and position them against the ends of the upstands. Wait for the glue to harden and remove the upstands. Trim and sand the ends of the stops.

10. Sand, stain, and polish the top.

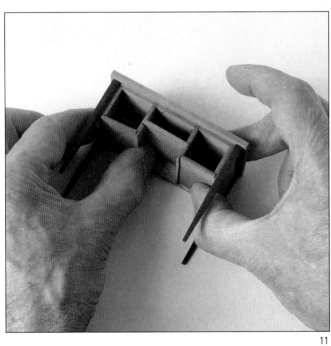

11. Check the alignment of the top and carcass against the assembled end panels and legs. Glue the end panels in position. The back legs should line up with the back of the carcass, the front legs should protrude slightly.

12. Glue the upstands in position.

M A K I N G   T H E   D R A W E R S

~

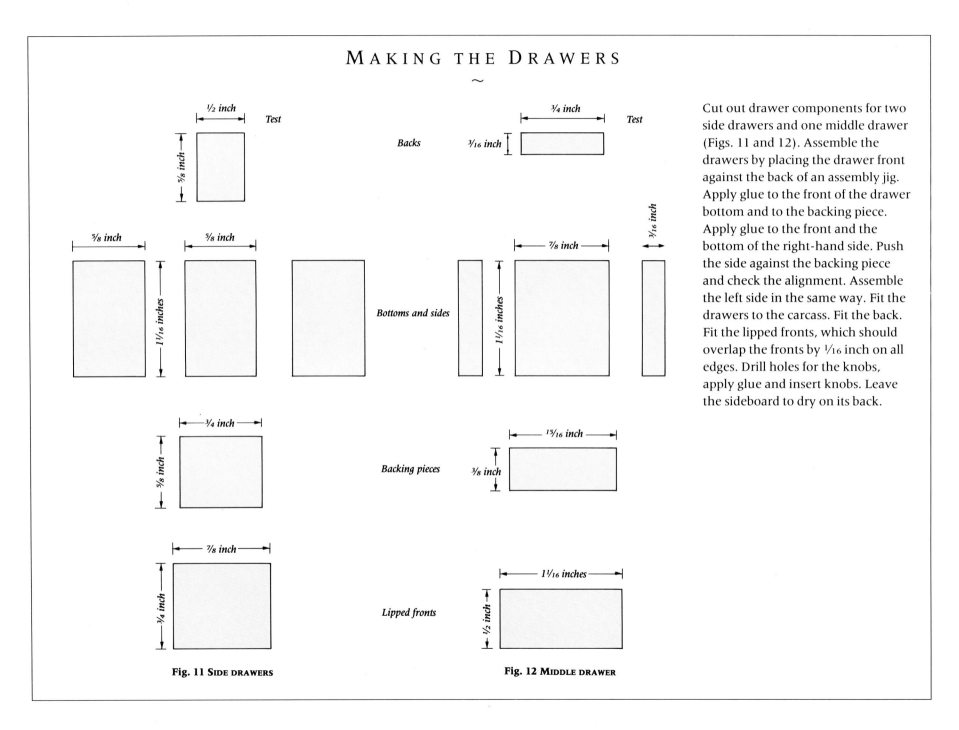

½ inch Test

Backs

¾ inch Test

³⁄₁₆ inch

⅝ inch

⅝ inch   ⅝ inch

7⁄8 inch

³⁄₁₆ inch

1¹⁄₁₆ inches

Bottoms and sides

1¹⁄₁₆ inches

¾ inch

Backing pieces

¹⁵⁄₁₆ inch

⅜ inch

⅝ inch

7⁄8 inch

Lipped fronts

1¹⁄₁₆ inches

¾ inch

½ inch

Fig. 11 SIDE DRAWERS

Fig. 12 MIDDLE DRAWER

Cut out drawer components for two side drawers and one middle drawer (Figs. 11 and 12). Assemble the drawers by placing the drawer front against the back of an assembly jig. Apply glue to the front of the drawer bottom and to the backing piece. Apply glue to the front and the bottom of the right-hand side. Push the side against the backing piece and check the alignment. Assemble the left side in the same way. Fit the drawers to the carcass. Fit the back. Fit the lipped fronts, which should overlap the fronts by ¹⁄₁₆ inch on all edges. Drill holes for the knobs, apply glue and insert knobs. Leave the sideboard to dry on its back.

Occasional Table

~

This small table uses exactly the same construction as the Regency dining table, but it has a round top and needs only one leg, which is smaller than those on the dining table. The elegant design makes the table a splendid addition to any formal living room.

~

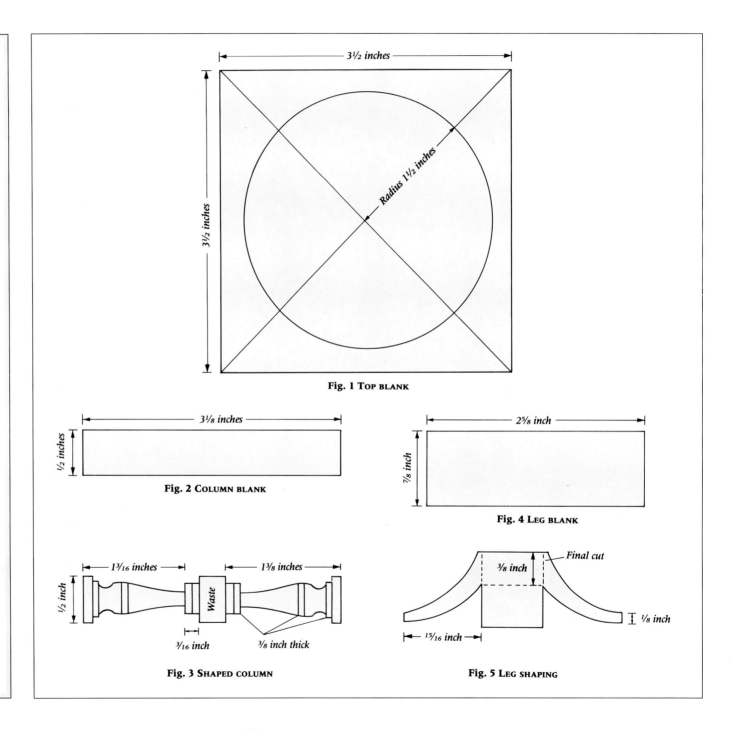

Fig. 1 TOP BLANK

Fig. 2 COLUMN BLANK

Fig. 4 LEG BLANK

Fig. 3 SHAPED COLUMN

Fig. 5 LEG SHAPING

1. Cut the circular table top to a radius of 1½ inches from a blank ⅛ inch thick. These four photographs show the stages of cutting the table top on a bandsaw using a circle cutting pin.

1A

1B

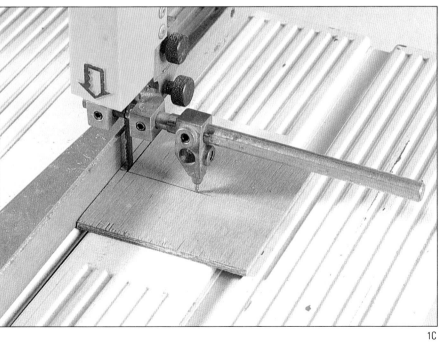

1C

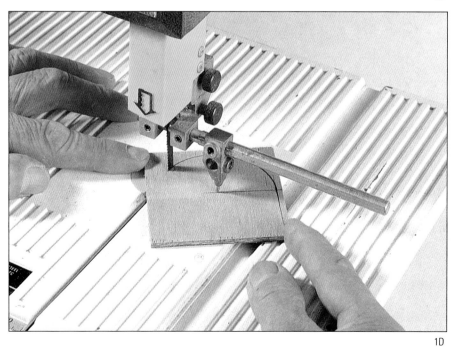

1D

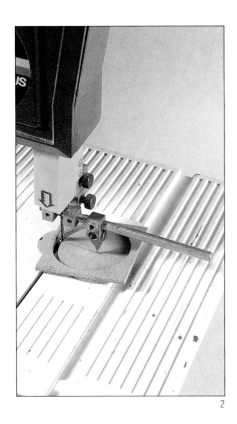

2. Completing the circle cut.

3. The cut table top and blocks for mounting it on the lathe.

4. Chamfer the edge of the table top. You can use a lathe if you have one, or simply sand the underside of the top. Finish by hand with medium and fine sandpaper.

5. The column, leg holder and legs are made in the same way as the Regency Dining Table; the only difference is that this column is shorter.

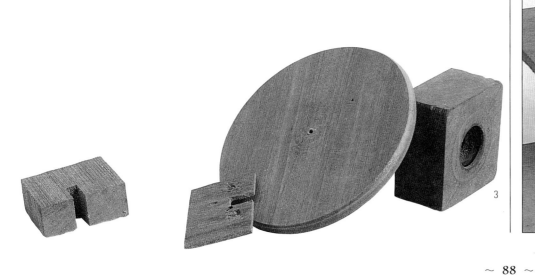

MAKING THE COLUMNS

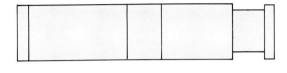

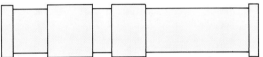

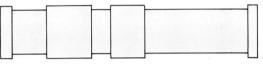

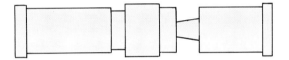

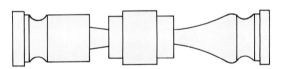

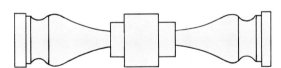

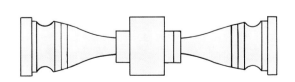

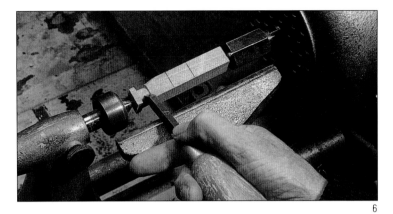

6. Cut a square-ended blank – one blank makes two columns – to the dimensions shown in Fig. 2. The leg column will then need to be shaped according to the sequence shown, but ending up with a column to the dimensions shown in Fig. 3.

7. Hand-sand the column. Cut the two top rings. Cut the ring on the pad. Dust, stain and French polish the column. Cut the column to its final length – 1³⁄₁₆ inches.

8. Glue the column to the center of the table top.

9. Dust, sand, and polish the table top.

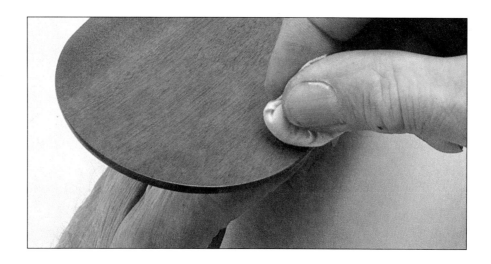

MAKING THE LEG HOLDERS
~

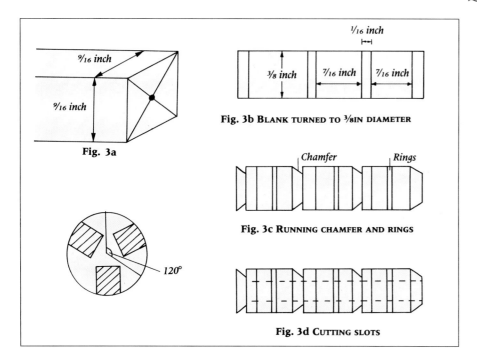

⁹/₁₆ inch

⁹/₁₆ inch

Fig. 3a

120°

¹/₁₆ inch

³/₈ inch *⁷/₁₆ inch* *⁷/₁₆ inch*

Fig. 3b BLANK TURNED TO ³/₈IN DIAMETER

Chamfer *Rings*

Fig. 3c RUNNING CHAMFER AND RINGS

Fig. 3d CUTTING SLOTS

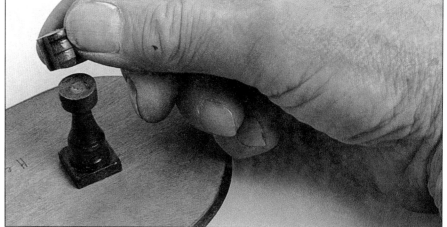

10. For the leg holder, cut a square-ended blank (Fig. 3a) and turn it so that it is ³/₈ inch in diameter (Fig. 3b). Cut rings and a chamfer (Fig. 3c). Stain and polish the pieces. Cut three slots down the sides of the piece at 120° to each other (Fig. 3d). Make the final cuts to give a length of ⁷/₁₆ inch. Assemble the leg holders to the columns.

10

11. You will need three legs for one table – a pair of legs is cut from one slice. You may want to use the pinned blank method (see page 10), illustrated here, to guarantee uniformity of the pieces you cut. Test the width of leg required against the slots cut in step 10, and cut the slices (Fig. 4) to this width. Glue the leg holder to the column. Draw the leg shape on a slice, or just the top slice if using pinned blank, and cut out the number of pieces required.

12. Sand the legs and attach them to the leg holders. The final assembly jig is, in principle, the same as for the Regency Dining Table, except that there is space for only one column and the height from the floor of the jig to the top surface is 1⅜ inches. Place the table in the assembly jig and leave to dry.

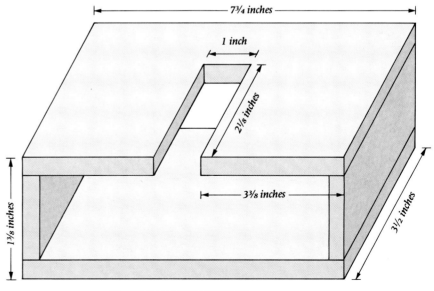

Fig. 12 OCCASIONAL TABLE JIG

11

RIGHT: *The Occasional Table*

Chesterfield Sofa

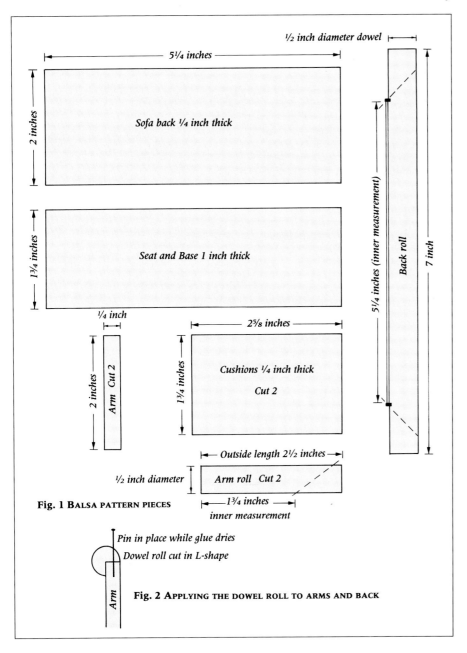

Fig. 1 BALSA PATTERN PIECES

½ inch diameter dowel

5¼ inches

Sofa back ¼ inch thick

2 inches

1¾ inches

Seat and Base 1 inch thick

¼ inch

2 inches   Arm Cut 2

2⅝ inches

1¾ inches   Cushions ¼ inch thick   Cut 2

5¼ inches (inner measurement)   Back roll   7 inch

Outside length 2½ inches

½ inch diameter   Arm roll Cut 2

1¾ inches
inner measurement

Pin in place while glue dries
Dowel roll cut in L-shape

Arm

Fig. 2 APPLYING THE DOWEL ROLL TO ARMS AND BACK

You Will Need
~

☛ Balsa wood for base 5¼ × 1¾ × 1inches; for back 5¼ × 2 × ¼ inches; for arms (cut 2) 2 × 2 × ¼ inches; for cushions (cut 2) 2⅝ × 1¾ × ¼ inches

☛ Sandpaper

☛ 15 inches dowel ½ inches in diameter

☛ Mat knife

☛ Wood glue

☛ 1 inch dressmaking pins

☛ Batting, approximately 8 × 8 inches

☛ Fabric for covering (lightweight wool, cotton or silk), approximately 9 inches

☛ Sewing thread

☛ Clear, all-purpose fabric adhesive

☛ 2 round-headed upholstery pins, ⅛ inch in diameter, for ends of arms

☛ Hardwood, 1 × 1 × ⅛ inch, cut into 4 squares for feet

1. Cut out the balsawood pieces. Smooth all the pieces with a sanding block. Sand the top edges of the two cushion pieces, rounding off the corners and shaving away a fraction on each edge so that they will fit onto the upholstered seat.

2. Cut the balsa dowel with the aid of a miter block into two arm rolls, each 2½ inches at the outer edge, and one back roll, 7 inches at the outer edge. If you do not have a miter block, draw a right angle with a carpenter's square on a wood-working board, divide the angle into 45° with a strong pencil line, and use this as a guide for your cutting angle. Use a mat knife to cut an L-shape out of the length of each piece of dowel (see Fig. 2).

3. Cut out the fabric pieces for the base (cut one), the back (cut one), and the arm pieces (cut two). Do not cut out the batting at this stage. Glue the fabric for the sofa seat and front of base into position, starting at the back edge of the balsa base. When the back edge is secure, smooth the fabric forward and down over the seat, and glue it under the base. Glue both arm covers to the arms, and then glue the back in the same way. Note that the fabric covers the outside surface, not the seat side, of the back. When the fabric covering is in position, glue the back of the sofa to the seat with wood glue. Clamp the pieces together until the glue is dry. Glue the arms in position. You can put dressmaking pins through the arms into the base to hold the arms.

4. Glue the rolls to the carcass. If the miter ends do not fit, sand any

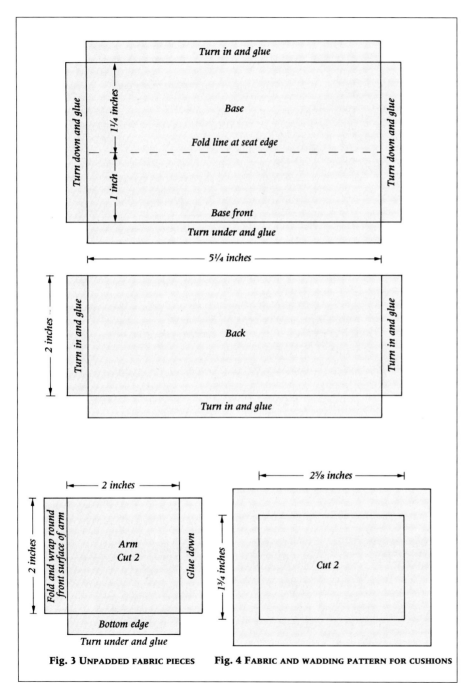

Fig. 3 UNPADDED FABRIC PIECES

Fig. 4 FABRIC AND WADDING PATTERN FOR CUSHIONS

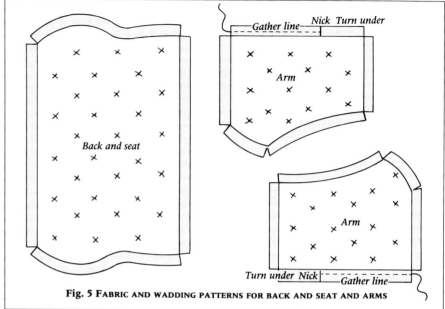

Fig. 5 FABRIC AND WADDING PATTERNS FOR BACK AND SEAT AND ARMS

excess or fill the gaps with a small piece of glue-soaked batting.

5. For the buttoned-effect version, cut out the batting and fabric pieces as shown in Figs. 4 and 5. Cut two cushion covers and two batting pieces. Note that the batting for the cushions should be cut exactly to size, with no allowance for edging. Draw the dots on the batting for the arms and back. These dots must be evenly spaced or the effect will be unsatisfactory. Baste the batting to the fabric for the arms and back, taking the batting stitches diagonally across the fabric, from corner to corner. Shave off a thickness of batting around all edges so that it is thinner along the gluing lines.

Beginning with the center line of dots on the back piece and using a darker-colored sewing thread, work horizontally in a zigzag stitch. Bring the needle through from the back of the fabric and across to the first dot. Pull the thread tight enough to form a slight swelling but not so tight that the fabric puckers. Secure with a small backstitch through the dot. Continue in this way until all the dots are joined (see Fig. 6). Turn under and baste down the seam allowances. Stitch the arms in the same way, but do not turn under the allowance at the top outside edge.

6. Place the back piece in position and make sure that it will fit, adjusting the hem allowance if necessary. Use fabric glue and dress-making pins to hold the back in position. When glued firmly, smooth the fabric piece forward over the roll and glue and pin it in place where the seat joins the sofa back. Allow glue to dry, remove pins. Cover the arms in the same way. Do not turn under the allowances on the outer arm edges above the notch marked. Catchstitch the turned-under edges, below the notch, to the edge of the arm front and fasten off. Take small gathering stitches along the arm roll edge, draw them up to form a rosette. Trim off any excess fabric before pushing in the upholstery pin. Catchstitch the fabric on the mitered corners together and fasten off.

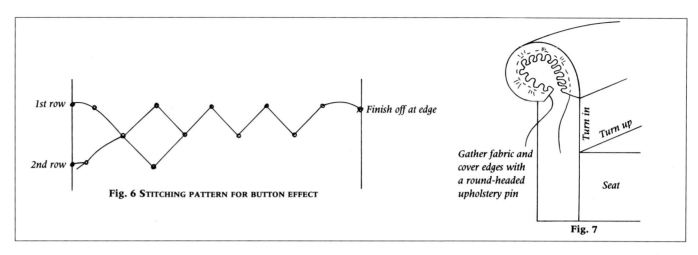

Fig. 6 STITCHING PATTERN FOR BUTTON EFFECT

1st row

2nd row

Finish off at edge

Gather fabric and cover edges with a round-headed upholstery pin

Turn in

Turn up

Seat

Fig. 7

7. Cut out the cushion cover pieces in fabric and batting. Check the balsa cushion pieces for fit against the upholstered sofa, sanding off the excess if necessary. Glue the piece of batting on the top of the cushion piece. Glue the back allowance of the fabric piece to the back of the balsa cushion, smoothing the fabric forwards over the batting and gluing it in position under the front edge. Allow the glue to dry. Bend over the side edges, smoothing the fullness of the corners neatly and evenly around and under. Glue in place.

8. If you do not want to make a buttoned version, baste the batting to the fabric and proceed as above. Remove all basting stitches when the fabric pieces are glued in place.

9. Glue the squares of hardwood to the corners of the sofa to form feet.

Footstool

You Will Need

~

- ⅛ inch wood, 1½ × 1 inches
- ³⁄₁₆ inch balsa wood, ⅞ × 1⅜ inches
- Tapestry, petit point or suitable fabric to cover, 2 × 1½ inches
- Thin batting, 1¾ × 1¼ inches
- Narrow trim (rickrack, cord or embossed paper), 5 inches
- 4 tiny, round-headed, brass- or copper-finish upholstery pins, with ⅛ inch heads for feet
- Fine sandpaper
- Wood glue
- Strong, non-staining fabric glue

1. Cut the base shape in wood and the smaller balsa wood shape. Soften the edges and corners of the balsa piece to make a cushion shape. Glue this to the wooden base.

2. Cut the batting shape and glue it to the balsa wood. Glue the shorter sides, stroking the batting out and down to achieve a smooth, taut surface. When it is firmly glued, stick down the longer sides. Use sharp scissors to snip away any excess so

that the batting does not overlap the base edges.

3. Cut the fabric pattern. First glue the shorter sides, bringing the fabric flush with the edge of the base wood. When the glue is dry, smooth the fabric across from the longer edge and press it flush with the side of the base wood. Do not overlap the fabric under the base (see Fig. 5). Trim away any excess so that it is flush with the base.

4. Glue trim around the base edge.

5. Press pins into the bottom of the base as indicated on Fig. 1. If the shanks are too long, trim them with wire cutters or pliers and add a dab of wood glue to the shank before pushing them in. You may need a spiral drill to make the pin holes. If you do not have one, heat a needle and burn holes; this will stop the wood from splitting.

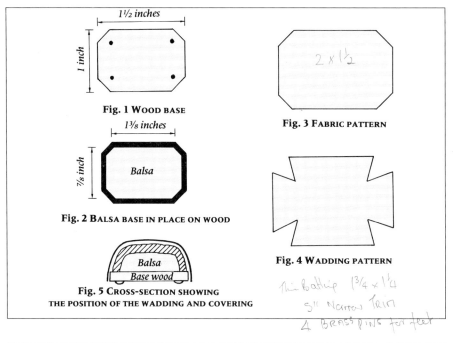

Fig. 1 WOOD BASE
1½ inches
1 inch

Fig. 3 FABRIC PATTERN
2 × 1½

Fig. 2 BALSA BASE IN PLACE ON WOOD
1⅜ inches
⅞ inch
Balsa

Fig. 4 WADDING PATTERN

Fig. 5 CROSS-SECTION SHOWING THE POSITION OF THE WADDING AND COVERING
Balsa
Base wood

Thin Batting 1¾ × 1¼
5" Narrow Trim
4 Brass Pins for feet